JOSHUA, JUDGES, & RUTH

Finally in the Land

John MacArthur

THOMAS NELSON
Since 1798

MacArthur Bible Studies

JOSHUA, JUDGES, & RUTH: FINALLY IN THE LAND

Published in Nashville, Tennessee, by Nelson Books, an imprint of Thomas Nelson. Nelson Books and Thomas Nelson are registered trademarks of HarperCollins Christian Publishing, Inc.

Originally published in association with the literary agency of Wolgemuth & Associates, Inc. Original layout, design, and writing assistance by Gregory C. Benoit Publishing, Old Mystic, Connecticut.

"Unleashing God's Truth, One Verse at a Time®" is a trademark of Grace to You. All rights reserved.

Thomas Nelson, Inc. titles may be purchased in bulk for educational, business, fundraising, or sales promotional use. For information, please e-mail SpecialMarkets@ThomasNelson.com.

ISBN 978-0-7180-3471-9

First Printing February 2016 / Printed in the United States of America

HB 10.26.2021

CONTENTS

Introduction   *v*

1. Investigating the Land   1
   Joshua 2:1–24

2. Crossing into Canaan   13
   Joshua 3:1–4:24

3. The Fall of Jericho   25
   Joshua 5:1–6:27

4. The Sin of Achan   37
   Joshua 7:1–8:35

5. The Sun Stands Still   49
   Joshua 9:1–10:25

6. Raising Up Judges   61
   Judges 1:1–2:23

7. Deborah and Barak   73
   Judges 4:1–5:31

8. Gideon and the Midianites   83
   Judges 6:1–40

9. Samson and the Philistines 95
Judges 15:1–16:31

10. Ruth and Boaz 107
Ruth 1:1–2:23

11. The Kinsman Redeemer 119
Ruth 3:1–4:22

12. Reviewing Key Principles 131

INTRODUCTION

After the exodus from Egypt, the people of Israel, now freed from slavery, wandered in the wilderness for forty years—but that was not the original plan. The people were supposed to go directly from the land of bondage into the Promised Land of Canaan. But they had been unwilling to trust God, so He waited until *an entire generation* died before leading the nation of Israel into Canaan.

Our studies open at the time when the Israelites are entering Canaan under the leadership of Joshua. Beginning with the crossing of the Jordan River, we will cover a span of many hundreds of years, culminating in the life and death of Samson. During this time period, we will discover two overriding themes: (1) God's people lived in a continuing cycle of sin and repentance, but (2) God was *always* faithful.

In these twelve studies, we will examine the biblical events depicted in the books of Joshua, Judges, and Ruth. We will look at the miraculous parting of the Jordan River, continue through some of Israel's victories and setbacks in the land of Canaan, and conclude with the people settling into the land during the time of the judges. We will study the lives of some of the Bible's heroes of the faith and the lives of a few of God's people who failed at times.

Through it all, you will learn some precious truths in this study about the character of God, and you will see His great faithfulness in keeping His promises. You will learn, in short, what it means to walk by faith.

The Book of Joshua

This is the first of twelve historical books in the Old Testament. It gained its name from the exploits of Joshua, the understudy whom Moses commissioned as a leader in Israel. *Joshua* means "Jehovah saves" or "the LORD is salvation," and corresponds to the New Testament name *Jesus*. God delivered Israel in Joshua's day when He was personally present as the saving commander who fought on Israel's behalf.

Author and Date

Although the author is not named, the most probable candidate is Joshua, who was the key eyewitness to the events. Joshua was born in Egyptian slavery, trained under Moses, and by God's choice rose to his key position of leading Israel into Canaan. An assistant whom Joshua groomed could have finished the book by attaching such comments as those concerning Joshua's death (see 24:29–33). Some have even suggested this section was written by the high priest Eleazar or his son, Phinehas. The book was completed before David's reign, and the most likely writing period is c. 1405–1385 BC.

Background and Setting

Israel was at the end of its forty-year wilderness wandering period (c. 1405 BC) when Moses passed the baton of leadership on to Joshua, who would have been approaching ninety years of age at the time. As the book opens, the Israelites are poised on the plains of Moab, east of the Jordan River and the land that God had promised. They faced peoples on the western side who had become so steeped in iniquity that God would cause the land to spew them out, so to speak (see Leviticus 18:24–25). God would give Israel the land by conquest, primarily to fulfill the covenant He had pledged to Abraham and his descendants, but also to pass just judgment on the sinful inhabitants.

Historical and Theological Themes

A keynote feature of the book is God's faithfulness to fulfill His promise of giving the land to Abraham's descendants. By His leading, the people inhabited the territories east and west of the Jordan River. Related to this theme is Israel's failure to press their conquest to every part of the land (Judges 1–2 later describes the tragic results from this sin). God wanted His people to possess the land (1) to keep His promise (see Genesis 12:7); (2) to set the stage for later developments in His kingdom plan (positioning Israel for events during the periods of the kings and prophets); (3) to punish those who were an affront to Him because of extreme sinfulness; and (4) to be a testimony to other peoples as God's covenant heart reached out to all nations.

INTERPRETIVE CHALLENGES

Miracles always challenge readers either to believe that the God who created heaven and earth can do other mighty works, or to explain them away. As in Moses' day, the miracles in this book were part of God's purpose, including (1) His holding back of the Jordan's waters (see Joshua 3:7–17); (2) the fall of Jericho's walls (see 6:1–27); (3) the hailstones (see 10:1–11); and (4) the long day (see 10:12–15). Other challenges include (1) how God's blessing on the harlot Rahab, who responded to Him in faith, related to her telling a lie; (2) why Achan's family members were executed with him; and (3) why Ai, with fewer men than Israel, was hard to conquer. These questions will be addressed in this study.

THE BOOK OF JUDGES

The book bears the fitting name *Judges*, which refers to the unique leaders God gave to His people to preserve them against their enemies. The Hebrew title means "deliverers" or "saviors," as well as judges. Twelve such judges arose before the time of Samuel, and then Eli and Samuel increased the count to fourteen. Judges spans about 350 years from Joshua's successful conquest (c. 1398 BC) until Eli and Samuel judged prior to the establishment of the monarchy (c. 1051 BC).

AUTHOR AND DATE

No author is named in the book, but the Jewish Talmud identifies Samuel, a key prophet who lived at the time these events took place. The date of composition was earlier than David's capture of Jerusalem (c. 1004 BC), since Jebusites still controlled the site. Also, the writer deals with a time before a king ruled. Saul began his reign c. 1051 BC, so a time shortly after his rule began is probably when Judges was written.

BACKGROUND AND SETTING

Judges is a tragic sequel to Joshua. In Joshua, the people were obedient to God in conquering the land. In Judges, they were disobedient, idolatrous, and often defeated. The account describes seven distinct cycles of Israel's drifting away from the Lord, starting even before Joshua's death and with a full departure into apostasy afterward. Five basic reasons are evident for these cycles of Israel's moral and spiritual decline: (1) failure to drive the Canaanites out of the land; (2) idolatry; (3) intermarriage with Canaanites; (4) not obeying the judges; and (5) turning away from God after the death of the judges. A four-part sequence repeatedly occurred during this phase of Israel's history: (1) Israel's departure from God; (2) God's judgment in permitting military defeat and subjugation; (3) Israel's prayer for deliverance; and (4) God raising up "judges" to lead in shaking off the oppressors.

HISTORICAL AND THEOLOGICAL THEMES

Judges is thematic rather than chronological. Foremost among its themes are God's power and His covenant mercy in graciously delivering the Israelites from the consequences of their failures, which were suffered for sinful compromise. In seven historical periods of sin to salvation, God compassionately delivered His people throughout the different geographical areas of tribal inheritances, which He had earlier given through Joshua. The apostasy covered the whole land, as indicated by the fact that each area was specifically identified. God's power to rescue shines brightly against the dark backdrop of human compromise and sometimes bizarre twists of sin.

INTERPRETIVE CHALLENGES

The most stimulating challenges of Judges are: (1) how to view men's violent acts against enemies or fellow countrymen; (2) God's use of leaders who, at times, did His will and, at other times, followed their own sinful impulses; (3) how to view Jephthah's vow and offering of his daughter (see 11:30–40); and (4) how to resolve God's sovereign will with His providential working in spite of human sin. The chronology of the various judges in different sectors of the land raises questions about how much time passed and how the time totals fit into the entire time span from the exodus (c. 1445 BC) to Solomon's fourth year (c. 967/966 BC), which is said to be 480 years (see 1 Kings 6:1). A reasonable explanation is that the deliverances and years of rest under the judges included overlaps, so that some of them ran concurrently.

THE BOOK OF RUTH

Ancient versions and modern translations consistently entitle this book after Ruth the Moabitess heroine, who is mentioned by name twelve times. The Old Testament does not again refer to Ruth, while the New Testament mentions her just once in the context of Christ's genealogy (see Matthew 1:5). *Ruth* most likely comes from a Moabite and/or Hebrew word meaning "friendship." Ruth arrived in Bethlehem as a foreigner, became a maidservant, married wealthy Boaz, and was an important link in the physical lineage of Christ.

AUTHOR AND DATE

Jewish tradition credits Samuel as the author, which is plausible as he did not die until after he had anointed David as God's chosen king. However, neither internal features nor external testimony conclusively identifies the writer. This exquisite story most likely appeared shortly before or during David's reign of Israel (1011–971 BC), since David is mentioned but not Solomon. Goethe reportedly labeled this piece of anonymous but distinguished literature as "the loveliest complete work on a small scale."

BACKGROUND AND SETTING

Aside from Bethlehem, the only other mentioned geographic/national entity is Moab, the perennial enemy of Israel located east of the Dead Sea. This country originated when Lot fathered Moab by an incestuous union with his oldest daughter (see Genesis. 19:37). Centuries later, the Jews encountered opposition from Balak, king of Moab, through the prophet Balaam (see Numbers 22–25), and then Moab oppressed Israel for eighteen years during the time of the judges. The story of Ruth occurred during those days (c. 1370 to 1041 BC) and thus bridges the time from the judges to Israel's monarchy.

Ruth 1:1 states that God used "a famine in the land" of Judah to set in motion this beautiful drama. However, this famine is not mentioned in Judges, which causes difficulty in dating the events. However, by working backward in time from the well-known date of David's reign (1011–971 BC), the time period of Ruth would most likely be during the judgeship of Jair, c. 1126–1105 BC. Ruth covers about eleven to twelve years according to the following scenario: (1) ten years in Moab (see 1:1–18); (2) several months (mid-April to mid-June) in Boaz's field (see 1:19–2:23); (3) one day in Bethlehem and one night at the threshing floor (see 3:1–18); and (4) about one year in Bethlehem (see 4:1–22).

HISTORICAL AND THEOLOGICAL THEMES

Ruth has been accepted as canonical by the Jews. Along with Song of Solomon, Esther, Ecclesiastes, and Lamentations, it stands with the Old Testament books of the Megilloth or "five scrolls." Rabbis read these books in the synagogue on five special occasions during the year—with Ruth being read at Jewish Pentecost due to the harvest scenes in Ruth 2–3. Genealogically, Ruth looks back almost nine hundred years to events during the time of Jacob and forward about one hundred years to the coming reign of David. While Joshua and Judges emphasize the legacy of the nation and their land of promise, Ruth focuses on the lineage of David back to the patriarchal era.

Seven major theological themes emerge in Ruth: (1) God's redemptive plan extends beyond the Jews; (2) women are coheirs with men of God's salvation grace; (3) Ruth portrays the virtuous woman of Proverbs 31:10; (4) God's sovereign and providential care of seemingly unimportant people at apparently insignificant times later proves to be crucial to accomplishing his will; (5) Ruth, along with Tamar, Rahab, and Bathsheba, stand in the genealogy of the messianic line; (6) Boaz, as a type of Christ, becomes Ruth's kinsman redeemer; (7) David's right (and thus Christ's right) to the throne of Israel is traced back to Judah.

INTERPRETIVE CHALLENGES

Ruth should be understood as a true historical account. The reliable facts surrounding Ruth, in addition to its complete compatibility with Judges and 1–2 Samuel, confirm Ruth's authenticity. However, some difficulties require careful attention. First, how could Ruth worship at the tabernacle in Shiloh, as the Law forbade Moabites from entering the assembly for ten generations? The answer can be found in the fact the Jews entered the land c. 1405 and Ruth was not born until c. 1150 BC, which means she represented at least the eleventh generation if the time limitation ended at ten generations. If "ten generations" was an idiom meaning "forever" (as Nehemiah 13:1 implies), then Ruth would be like the foreigner of Isaiah 56:1–8 who joined himself to the Lord, thus gaining entrance to the assembly.

Second, are there not immoral overtones to Boaz and Ruth spending the night together before marriage (see 3:3–18)? In fact, Ruth engaged in a common ancient Near Eastern custom by asking Boaz to take her for his wife, as symbolically pictured by throwing a garment of love and care over the intended woman. The text does not even hint at the slightest moral impropriety, noting that Ruth slept at his feet.

Third, would not the levirate principle of Deuteronomy 25:5–6 lead to incest and/or polygamy if the nearest relative was already married? In truth, God would not design a good plan to involve the grossest of immoralities punishable by death. Implementation of Deuteronomy 25:5–6 could involve only the nearest relative who was eligible for marriage as qualified by other stipulations of the Law.

Finally, was marriage to a Moabitess not strictly forbidden by the Law? The answer to this question is found in the fact that the nations to whom marriage was prohibited were those possessing the land Israel would enter, which did not include Moab. Further, Boaz married Ruth, a devout proselyte to Yahweh (see 1:16–17), not a pagan worshiper of Moab's deities.

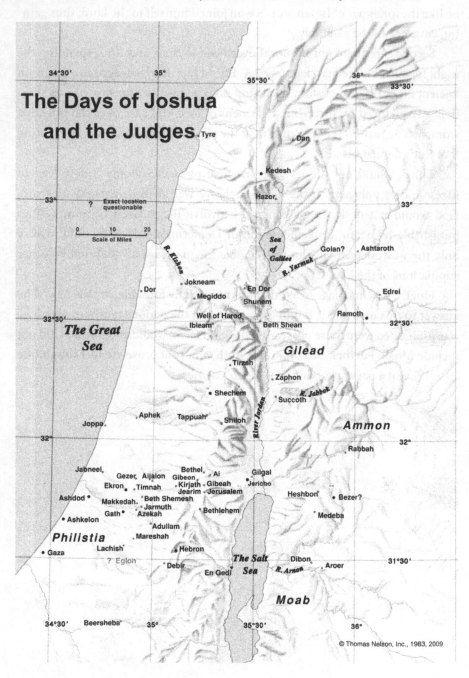

The Days of Joshua and the Judges

INVESTIGATING THE LAND

Joshua 2:1–24

DRAWING NEAR

Name one situation in your life in which you had to completely put your faith in someone or something. How did that turn out for you?

_____

_____

_____

THE CONTEXT

At the close of the book of Numbers, the Israelites were nearing the end of their forty years of wandering in the wilderness. They had destroyed several Canaanite armies, and the Lord's power had become evident to the nations around them. Joshua had led the people to an acacia grove on the east side of the Jordan River, where they prepared to enter the land of Canaan. The first stronghold that stood in their way was the city of Jericho.

Joshua was a strong military leader and wanted information about Jericho prior to facing the city in battle. So, to gain that information, he sent two spies into the city to learn more about its inhabitants and their defenses. We are not told what those spies learned, because in the long run it didn't matter. God's plans for Jericho's destruction did not require any military prowess or human strategies. He would use supernatural means to destroy His enemies. But He would also bring salvation to one particular person who lived in that city, and He would use the spies to reach her.

Jericho was surrounded by two walls, one behind the other. Between those walls were houses that were actually built into one or both walls, and those houses frequently had windows that opened through the city's defensive walls. Such houses were simple and small, inhabited by the city's poor—and worse. Their location near the city gates, for example, would be a perfect place to carry on the business of prostitution. The constant traffic of people entering and leaving the city would be good for business, especially since it would be easy to enter and exit such a house unnoticed. This element of anonymity was also useful for the spies, as it was unlikely they would be noticed entering such a house of prostitution.

In the book of Joshua we will see God work some powerful and dramatic miracles, beginning with the parting of the Jordan River. However, in this study we will witness a miracle of even greater power and drama: the Lord will redeem the life of a lowly Canaanite prostitute. In fact, He will go beyond that miracle and transform this woman of sin into a woman of God—and her descendants will include Jesus Himself.

KEYS TO THE TEXT

Read Joshua 2:1–24, noting the key words and phrases indicated below.

> SPIES IN JERICHO: *Joshua begins the conquest of the Promised Land by sending two spies into the strategic city of Jericho to gather information. The spies hide in the house of a prostitute.*

2:1. ACACIA GROVE: This grove was on the east side of the river and was used as a base camp.

CAME TO THE HOUSE OF A HARLOT: The two spies did not visit Rahab's house for any illicit purpose but rather because it offered a good hiding place. They were spies of a hostile army, and as such were at risk of losing their lives if caught. They probably thought that strange men entering a prostitute's house would not be noticed. However, it was actually the Lord Himself who led them there, because He intended to rescue Rahab and redeem her.

4. HID THEM: At this point, Rahab made a risky decision from which

there was no turning back. She would have been immediately put to death if the men had been discovered in her house. She had already made up her mind to join Israel and make their God her God.

5. THE MEN WENT OUT: Rahab lied in order to protect the two Israelites, and in so doing probably considered it justified during a time of war. In the Lord's eyes, the ends do not justify the means—lying is a sin, and He never condones it. Nevertheless, God focused on Rahab's faith and her courageous decision to help His people.

6. HIDDEN THEM WITH THE STALKS OF FLAX: Houses in those days had flat roofs that were used for many purposes, including as places to dry grains. Flax was used to make linen cloth.

TURNING TO GOD: Rahab saves the spies because she recognizes that Israel serves the only true God, the Creator of heaven and earth.

9. I KNOW THAT THE LORD HAS GIVEN YOU THE LAND: Rahab revealed her motivation in what she said to the spies. Notice that she mentioned the Lord's name repeatedly. She recognized that Israel's great victories were the work of God, not of men, and she wanted to make peace with Israel's God. In this, she was far wiser than the kings of Canaan.

11. THE LORD YOUR GOD, HE IS GOD IN HEAVEN ABOVE AND ON EARTH BENEATH: This was a profound confession of faith in God. Rahab helped the Israelites because she recognized that their God was the one true God. This was the faith the New Testament writers commended, and it is a testimony to God's grace that even a prostitute could be saved. God did not want to send judgment on the people of Canaan. The tragedy of this passage is that there were so few who repented like Rahab and so many who fought against the God of Israel to the bitter end.

12. SWEAR TO ME BY THE LORD: Rahab also recognized there was no higher oath that God's people could swear than one sworn by His name. The spies would have brought grave dishonor on the Lord's name if they had failed to keep their promise. Rahab already understood the Lord was faithful to keep His promises, so she knew that an oath given in His name by His people would be binding. Later, the Lord would again honor such a promise, given by the Israelites to the people of Gibeon (see Joshua 9:18), even though it would be made without consulting Him.

3

13. SPARE MY FATHER, MY MOTHER, MY BROTHERS, MY SISTERS: Rahab was not thinking only of herself in this time of crisis. She made it a point to also save the lives of her entire family.

THE SCARLET THREAD: The spies instruct Rahab how to save herself and her family from the coming destruction by using a scarlet thread. This thread serves to remind us of the Passover sacrifice.

15. SHE DWELT ON THE WALL: Jericho, like other cities of the time, was surrounded by two concentric walls, the inner wall standing on higher ground than the outer one. Frequently there were houses built between those walls, often with windows opening out of the walls themselves. Rahab probably dropped a rope through her window, down the front side of the outer wall, to the ground below. This was an immensely risky undertaking, as the rope and the spies would have been in plain sight. Even at night there would have been a great risk of being caught. The Lord was protecting His people from detection.

18. BIND THIS LINE OF SCARLET CORD IN THE WINDOW: There was a practical sense to the scarlet cord, as its color made it easily visible against the brown mud walls of the city. But there was also an important symbolic significance in the scarlet cord, as its blood-red color pointed ahead to the final atonement of Christ. Rahab hung the cord from her window, much as the Israelites had painted their doorposts with the blood of the Passover lambs prior to leaving Egypt (see Exodus 12). During the Passover, the Lord sent an angel throughout Egypt to slay the firstborn son of any household that was not covered by the blood of a sacrificed lamb. Anyone who was inside a house covered by the blood was safe from death—just as Rahab's family would only be safe if they remained inside her house when God's destruction came on Jericho.

GOING DEEPER

Read Hebrews 11:24–31, noting the key words and phrases indicated below.

BY FAITH: The author of Hebrews gives many examples from the Old Testament of people who lived by faith—and Rahab is among them.

11:24. BY FAITH: Hebrews 11 is commonly referred to as the "faith chapter" because it lists many great heroes of faith from the Old Testament. The central theme of this chapter is the fact that service to God requires faith, for "without faith it is impossible to please Him, for he who comes to God must believe that He is, and that He is a rewarder of those who diligently seek Him" (verse 6). The author of Hebrews defines faith as "the substance of things hoped for, the evidence of things not seen" (verse 1). The person of faith chooses to believe in that which is "not seen" simply because God has promised it is true.

REFUSED TO BE CALLED THE SON OF PHARAOH'S DAUGHTER: Moses had every possible blessing this world affords, as he grew up in the royal court of the world's most powerful nation in his day. Rahab probably did not have much in terms of the world's wealth, but she did have a secure home inside the walls of a safe and powerful city. The heroes of the faith were people who saw beyond what the world had to offer and instead fixed their eyes on eternity. Rahab knew that her city was doomed simply because she believed God had the power to bring down those city walls. Like Moses, she refused to place her faith in the fortifications of mankind, choosing instead to trust in the protection and faithfulness of God.

30. BY FAITH THE WALLS OF JERICHO FELL DOWN: As we will discuss in a later study, God would reward Rahab's faith by keeping her and her family completely safe when He brought down the walls of Jericho. It would actually be the faith of the people of Israel that would bring down those walls, in the sense that they obeyed God's command to march around the city each day. The Lord would use their faithful obedience to work His own powerful miracle. God's people today are likewise called to live in faithful obedience.

Read James 2:19–26, noting the key words and phrases indicated below.

FAITH WITHOUT WORKS: James tells us how to determine whether our faith is alive or dead. A living faith is demonstrated by good works.

2:19. EVEN THE DEMONS BELIEVE: James noted that faith is not a mere mental acknowledgment of the facts concerning Christ, for even the demons believe there is one God who created the heavens and the earth—but that "faith" does not save them. True saving faith is active—being given and energized by the Holy Spirit—and transforms true believers from the inside out so that they desire to submit themselves to God and His Word. James was not suggesting that salvation is somehow based on a person's works; rather, he argued that true faith—that which is alive and powerful—would inevitably bear fruit of repentance and righteousness in the lives of those who possess it. We see this in the story of the kings of Canaan, who believed Israel's God was powerful and was leading His people to victory but did not allow that understanding to motivate them to submit to Him. Rahab's actions, however, demonstrated that her faith was genuine, for she openly forsook her former gods and embraced the Lord of creation.

20. FAITH WITHOUT WORKS IS DEAD: A faith that does not lead to repentance and obedience is a "dead faith." However, a faith that characterizes repentance and salvation is a "living faith," as made evident by fruits of obedience. Although salvation is found in Christ alone by grace alone through faith alone, those who have been genuinely saved (having been transformed by the regenerating work of the Holy Spirit) will subsequently show evidence of their faith and love for God in how they live.

21. JUSTIFIED BY WORKS: Again, James was not suggesting that we gain eternal life and peace with God by doing good works or being good people. On the contrary, once we are saved and indwelt by the Holy Spirit, our faith compels us to do good works. After all, our hearts and affections have been changed such that we who were formerly enemies of God now long to honor Him. Abraham believed God's promises that he would have a son, and that his son would produce as many descendants as the sands of the sea. When God commanded him to slay that son when the boy was still young, he must have wondered how God's promises could come to pass. Yet Abraham's faith in God's promises gave him the ability to obey—and in this sense the genuineness of his faith was proven and made evident by his actions.

25. WAS NOT RAHAB THE HARLOT ALSO JUSTIFIED BY WORKS: In the same way, Rahab had faith that God would save her and her family, and that faith led to the action of helping the spies and placing the scarlet cord in her window. The king of Jericho assented that Israel's God was mighty and faithful to His people, but his "faith" was dead, for it led him to run from God and to shut up the city against Israel's approach.

UNLEASHING THE TEXT

1) Why did the spies hide in the house of a prostitute? How was this a strategic move?

_____

_____

_____

2) What was Rahab's motivation in helping the spies? What did she hope to get out of it?

_____

_____

_____

3) Why did the spies order Rahab to bind a scarlet thread in her window? In what ways is this thread a symbol of salvation?

_____

_____

_____

4) In what ways was God's hand guiding the events in Rahab's life? What was His purpose for her? For the spies?

_____

_____

_____

EXPLORING THE MEANING

We are saved by faith, but that faith always leads to righteous behavior. James drew a strong distinction between genuine saving faith and mere intellectual acceptance of God's existence. As he pointed out, the demons themselves believe in the existence of God, and they tremble at that knowledge. One might go so far as to say the devil's understanding of God is orthodox: he acknowledges that God is one and that Jesus Christ is His Son who takes away the sins of the world. But that knowledge will not save the devil and his demons.

Mere knowledge about God is not enough to save a person. The person who recognizes that God exists and created the world does well, yet even the demons exhibit that amount of faith. The faith that saves is an active faith—a faith that leads a person to actively repent of sin and begin to enthusiastically obey the Word of God.

A faith that does not produce fruits of righteous behavior is a dead faith, because a living faith—the kind that saves—will always lead us to obey God's Word out of a heart that has been changed and now desires to please Him. As the apostle John wrote, "Now by this we know that we know Him, if we keep His commandments. He who says, 'I know Him,' and does not keep His commandments, is a liar, and the truth is not in him. But whoever keeps His word, truly the love of God is perfected in him. By this we know that we are in Him. He who says he abides in Him ought himself also to walk just as He walked" (1 John 2:3–6).

God's grace is freely available to everyone, no matter what has happened in the past. We know nothing about Rahab's life before she met the spies, but it was obviously filled with all manner of wickedness. She was in the lowest stratum of the city—an unclean woman who quite literally lived on the outskirts of society. If anyone was unfit for the kingdom of God, it was Rahab, and yet God redeemed her. More than that, He elevated her from the dregs of society to the highest of honors: her descendants culminated in the person of Jesus Christ.

Everyone has sinned and fallen short of the glory of God (see Romans 3:23), and one sin is just as grievous as another in God's eyes. The prostitute is no more unfit for God's kingdom than the law-abiding citizen, for all people are equally in need of God's forgiveness and grace. That's the bad news. The good news is that God has made forgiveness available to everyone who believes in Him—to the worst of sinners as well as the person who has lived a "good life."

The best news is that God's grace is freely available and there is nothing anyone can do to earn it or deserve it. Rahab did not deserve to be saved, yet God, in His grace, chose to rescue her and her family from certain destruction. Similarly, through the cross, God has made eternal salvation available to sinners who do not deserve it. He offers it freely to all who would repent of their sins and embrace in faith His Son, Jesus Christ.

God transforms sinners into saints. As we have just stated, Rahab was a grievous sinner who deliberately disobeyed God's commands for leading a righteous life. It was a tremendous act of grace for God to save her from judgment, but He did far more than that. He transformed her into a woman of God and placed her in the lineage of Christ.

Saul of Tarsus was also a grievous sinner. He spent his adult life persecuting the early Christian church, hunting down and arresting anyone who professed faith in Jesus. He was instrumental in putting Christians to death and assisting those who stoned them (see Acts 9:1–2). Yet God saved him, gave him a new name, and transformed him into an apostle whose writings fill the New Testament.

Our salvation is merely the first step in God's amazing work of redemption. When we repent of our sins and embrace God's grace through faith in Jesus Christ, we receive the inestimable gift of eternal life and also the gift of the Holy Spirit. The Spirit immediately begins the work of transformation in our lives, gradually making us more like Jesus Christ. This ultimate act of transformation exceeds even that done in Rahab's life, for the lowliest of sinners will one day reflect the full glory of God's Son, Jesus!

REFLECTING ON THE TEXT

5) Was it right or wrong for Rahab to lie about the spies? How might she have handled the situation without lying?

_____

_____

_____

6) What exactly is faith? Why is faith necessary if we are to please God?

_____

_____

_____

7) What is the difference between a living faith and a dead faith? How did Rahab demonstrate a living faith? How did the king of Jericho demonstrate a dead faith?

_____

_____

_____

8) Have you accepted God's free gift of salvation by placing your faith in His Son, Jesus Christ? If not, what is preventing you from doing so now?

_____

_____

_____

PERSONAL RESPONSE

9) In what ways has the Lord transformed you since you became a Christian? What transformations is He working on at present?

_____

_____

_____

10) Is your faith a living one? Are you walking in obedience to God's Word? What areas of obedience might the Lord be calling you to work on this week?

_____

_____

_____

2

CROSSING INTO CANAAN
Joshua 3:1–4:24

DRAWING NEAR

The Israelites took a step of faith into the Jordan River and crossed over on dry land. What is a "step of faith" you have taken in your life?

_____

_____

_____

THE CONTEXT

In the last study, we saw that Joshua had sent two spies into the city of Jericho to investigate its inhabitants and judge its defenses. During the course of their mission, they met a prostitute named Rahab, who recognized that the God they served would deliver Canaan into their hands. She said, "We have heard how the LORD dried up the water of the Red Sea for you when you came out of Egypt, and what you did to the two kings of the Amorites who were on the other side of the Jordan . . . And as soon as we heard these things, our hearts melted" (Joshua 2:10–11).

God had indeed not only performed great miracles for the Israelites but had also promised to drive out their enemies before their arrival into the

Promised Land. He had led them out of Egypt, defeated the armies of Pharaoh, and provided them with food and water in the wilderness. He had given them the Law and led them to the very doorstep of Canaan. But at that point the people's trust in God had faltered, and as a result the Lord had decreed that the entire generation would not enter the Promised Land.

Joshua had been present that fateful day when the people rebelled. He and Caleb had urged them to obey the Lord's command and continue forward into Canaan—which is the very reason God chose him to succeed Moses. Now, as the people again stood on the banks of the Jordan River, they vowed not to make the same mistakes. "All that you command us we will do," they said to Joshua, "and wherever you send us we will go. Just as we heeded Moses in all things, so we will heed you" (Joshua 1:16–17).

This time, the people will obey the Lord and take the first step of faith across the riverbed into Canaan. They know the situation in the Promised Land has not changed—there will still be many powerful adversaries to face—but the condition of their hearts has dramatically improved. This time, they will trust in the Lord, remember His great faithfulness to them, and pass the stories of God's faithfulness to future generations. They recognize they must not forget what the Lord has done for them, as the previous generation did, and see to it that their children don't forget either.

KEYS TO THE TEXT

Read Joshua 3:1–4:24, noting the key words and phrases indicated below.

> *GATHERING AT THE RIVER: The two spies Joshua sent to investigate Jericho have returned. Joshua now prepares the people to cross the Jordan River into Canaan.*

3:1. JOSHUA: Joshua had served for years as Moses' assistant and had also been one of twelve men originally sent into Canaan to spy out the land. Because he and Caleb had urged the people to obey God by crossing the Jordan into Canaan, the Lord rewarded them by permitting them to enter the Promised Land—while the rest of their generation died in the wilderness (see Numbers 13–14). Now, as this chapter opens, Joshua, Caleb, and the next generation of Israelites are preparing to enter Canaan.

3. THE ARK OF THE COVENANT: The ark was a sacred chest the Lord had commanded the Israelites to build when they first left Egypt. It was an ornate work of art made of acacia wood, approximately four feet in length, and a little more than two feet high and deep, topped with gorgeous carved angels, and overlaid in gold—inside and outside (see Exodus 25). The ark contained the tablets of the Ten Commandments as well as Aaron's rod and other symbols of God's deliverance from Egypt. Yet what made the ark so sacred to the Israelites was the fact that it represented the very presence of God. The carved angels atop the ark symbolized the mercy seat, the place where God's glorious presence was made manifest to Israel. The ark itself pictured the throne of God.

THE PRIESTS . . . BEARING IT: The ark was supported on two long poles and carried on the shoulders of four priests, one at each end of the poles.

4. THERE SHALL BE A SPACE BETWEEN YOU AND IT: The people were commanded to stay back roughly a thousand yards from the ark on their journey across the Jordan. (A cubit is approximately eighteen inches.) This was a sign of reverence for the presence of God, as the ark signified that He was with His people. The ark itself was to be treated with care and respect. Kohathites customarily carried the ark (see Numbers 4:15), but in this unusual case the Levitical priests transported it. No one was allowed to touch the ark.

THAT YOU MAY KNOW THE WAY: Another reason the people were to stay back from the ark was to permit all the people to see it. Because the ark visually indicated that God was leading the people, He wanted everyone to be able to freely view the symbol of His presence. It was important for the people to remember they were following God rather than men as they entered new territory, because they had forgotten that fact many times in the past. Whenever God's people forgot that He was in sovereign control of their circumstances, they became afraid and rebelled against His leadership. We tend to do the same today.

SANCTIFY YOURSELVES: *The Lord commands the people to prepare themselves, for they are about to see His power demonstrated in a very dramatic way.*

5. SANCTIFY YOURSELVES: Sinful mankind cannot enter the holy presence of the Lord, so the Israelites were commanded to purify themselves in preparation for moving forward with God's presence. The Lord had provided detailed instructions on how the Israelites were to keep themselves pure, as

well as instructions on how to consecrate themselves when something (such as contact with a dead body) had made them ceremonially impure. These rites and procedures, however, were only outward ways of addressing mankind's sinful condition; an animal sacrifice could not fully atone for anyone's sin. Today, Christians are fully forgiven and sanctified on the basis of Christ's once-for-all sacrifice. Even so, we are called, like ancient Israel, to keep our lives pure and to live as consecrated people.

6. CROSS OVER: That is, cross over the Jordan River.

8. STAND IN THE JORDAN: The priests were to take a visible stand in the middle of the Jordan River so the entire nation could see them. This would allow time for the people to reflect on God's greatness in giving them the land and prepare them for the miracle that was about to occur. The priests were the ones chosen to approach the insurmountable barrier that stood between Israel and the Promised Land, symbolically opening the way for Israel to cross. The Lord Jesus would also one day stand in the Jordan River to be baptized as He began His earthly ministry (see Matthew 3). He was the one who would finally remove the barrier that stood between mankind and God—the barrier of sin—and He would remove it *forever*.

10. DRIVE OUT FROM BEFORE YOU: This was an important reminder for the people of Israel, because the last time they had arrived at Jordan's banks, they had determined they could not defeat the Canaanites—which was true, as far as their own strength was concerned. Joshua needed to remind them not to be afraid, but instead to place their trust in God's power. The Canaanite people to be killed or defeated were extremely sinful. The question is not why God chose to destroy these sinners, but why He had let them live so long, and why all sinners are not destroyed far sooner than they are. It is grace that allows any sinner to draw one more breath of life.

CANAANITES: Broadly speaking, these were the descendants of Canaan, son of Ham, son of Noah (see Genesis 10:15–18), and included many of the other groups named in this verse.

HITTITES: Immigrants from the Hittite Empire (in the region of Syria) to the central region of the land.

HIVITES: Descendants of Canaan who lived in the northern reaches of the land.

PERIZZITES: People included among the general population of the land who did not trace their lineage to Canaan. Their exact identity is uncertain.

GIRGASHITES: A tribe descended from Canaan, which was included among the general population of the land without specific geographical identity.

AMORITES: A general term for the inhabitants of the land, but especially for the descendants of Canaan who inhabited the hill country on both sides of the Jordan.

JEBUSITES: Descendants of Canaan who dwelt in the hill country around Jerusalem.

16. ADAM: Approximately fifteen miles north on the Jordan River. See the map in the Introduction.

THE WATERS . . . WERE CUT OFF: The Lord had worked a similar miracle when the Israelites crossed the Red Sea under the leadership of Moses, more than forty years earlier (see Exodus 14). The Lord was reiterating for the people that He would remove any obstacle that stood between them and their inheritance in Canaan. He was also showing the Israelites that Joshua was His chosen leader, just as Moses had been previously.

17. ALL ISRAEL CROSSED OVER ON DRY GROUND: Once again, the Israelites were able to cross a body of water that moments before had stood as a barrier between them and the Promised Land. They crossed without even getting their feet wet, for the Lord did all the work on their behalf.

SET UP A MEMORIAL: *Twelve men—one from each tribe—carry a large stone on their shoulders out of the Jordan riverbed. The stones will serve as a memorial.*

4:2. TWELVE MEN: Moses had sent twelve men, one from each tribe, into Canaan some four decades previously to spy out the land. This time, rather than spying out the fortifications of the enemy, the Lord commanded the twelve to set up a memorial to what He had done—and would do—for them. The Lord was teaching His people to focus on His power and faithfulness, not on the obstacles that stood against them.

3. OUT OF THE MIDST OF THE JORDAN: The twelve stones were selected from the bed of the Jordan River rather than its banks. This would stand as proof to future generations that Israel had walked across the river on dry ground.

5. A STONE ON HIS SHOULDER: These stones were evidently quite large.

6. WHEN YOUR CHILDREN ASK IN TIME TO COME: Here the Lord was instructing His people on how to teach their children about His character.

Previously, Moses had taught them this same lesson when he said, "Take heed to yourself, and diligently keep yourself, lest you forget the things your eyes have seen, and lest they depart from your heart all the days of your life. And teach them to your children and your grandchildren" (Deuteronomy 4:9).

7. THESE STONES SHALL BE FOR A MEMORIAL: The people of Israel had demonstrated a tendency to forget about God's past blessings, particularly when faced with present obstacles. The Lord wants His people to *remember* His faithfulness, His great works of deliverance, His miraculous power—in short, to remember *Him*. For that reason, Jesus instituted a "remembrance feast" prior to His crucifixion that we know as the Lord's Supper.

THE PEOPLE OBEY: *A generation earlier, the Israelites had refused to obey the Lord's chosen leaders. This time, they willingly submit.*

8. JUST AS JOSHUA COMMANDED: Some forty years previous to this event, the people had been so adamant against Joshua and Caleb's wise counsel that they were ready to "stone them with stones" (Numbers 14:10). As we have seen, that entire generation had died out, and now the people were prepared to obey the Lord and submit to His appointed leader.

19. THE TENTH DAY OF THE FIRST MONTH: This was the day the Lord commanded Israel to kill a lamb in preparation for the tenth plague in Egypt; that is, the Passover Lamb (see Exodus 12:3). This day of Passover was important in the Jewish calendar (equating to March/April in our modern calendar), and it was the very day when Christ was crucified.

20. GILGAL: Approximately a mile from Jericho. See the map in the Introduction.

21. WHAT ARE THESE STONES: The memorial stones served several purposes. They reminded the people of what the Lord had done in their lives, and they also sparked questions from others, such as future children. The Israelites, like Christians today, were responsible not only to remember the Lord's grace but also to instill awe in their children concerning the things of God.

24. ALL THE PEOPLES OF THE EARTH MAY KNOW THE HAND OF THE LORD: Ultimately, the memorials were to serve as a testimony not merely to one's own family but to the entire world. Like Old Testament Israel, the church is to be a testimony of God's goodness, inciting a curiosity in the world around us and a hunger to know more about the God of our salvation.

UNLEASHING THE TEXT

1) If you had been traveling with the Israelites, how would you have reacted to crossing the Jordan River on dry ground?

_____

_____

_____

2) Why did the Lord command the Israelites to pile up twelve stones on the far side of the river? What things can we do, in our lives, to proactively remember God's faithfulness?

_____

_____

_____

3) Why did the Lord command one man from each tribe of Israel to carry a stone? How does this connect with God's commands to teach future generations?

_____

_____

_____

4) Why were the Israelites commanded to keep a great distance between themselves and the ark of the covenant?

_____

_____

_____

EXPLORING THE MEANING

God's people are to remember His faithfulness. As we have seen, God had performed many great miracles for His people. He had brought them out of Egypt, defeated Pharaoh's army, parted the Red Sea, and provided food and water for them in the wilderness. What's more, He had vowed to lead the Israelites safely into the Promised Land of Canaan. But the Israelites had lost heart when they reached the shores of the Jordan River and convinced themselves that their enemies were too powerful. They had refused to cross the river as God had instructed them to do. As a result of their disobedience, an entire generation died in the wilderness.

For this reason, the Lord commanded the next generation to set up a monument at the banks of the Jordan so they would never forget what He had done to lead them into the Promised Land. In the future, when they faced powerful enemies, they could look back at those twelve stones and remember what the Lord had done for them already. In this way, they could have courage to trust in Him for the future as well.

Jesus instituted a similar memorial before He went to Calvary by commanding His followers to break bread on a regular basis as a way of remembering what He had done to secure their salvation. "When He had given thanks, He broke [the unleavened bread] and said, 'Take, eat; this is My body which is broken for you; do this in remembrance of Me.' In the same manner He also took the cup after supper, saying, 'This cup is the new covenant in My blood. This do, as often as you drink it, in remembrance of Me.' For as often as you eat this bread and drink this cup, you proclaim the Lord's death till He comes" (1 Corinthians 11:24–26).

It is vital that Christians teach their children the things of God. The Lord reiterated several times that the memorial stones were to be a sign not just for the people of that generation but also for their children and their children's children—and to all future generations. The monument was intended to provoke questions from curious youngsters and to give parents an opportunity to tell their inquisitive children about all God had done for His people. However, as we will see in future studies, the people of Israel were not faithful in following these commands. Generation after generation would depart from the ways of the Lord because their parents had not effectively taught them to remember what God had done for His people.

In the book of Deuteronomy, Moses said to the people, "These words which I command you today shall be in your heart. You shall teach them diligently to your children, and shall talk of them when you sit in your house, when you walk by the way, when you lie down, and when you rise up" (6:6–7). There are many ways parents can teach their children: through words and actions, lifestyle and example, consistency and longevity. All of these elements are integral to teaching children, but another important aspect includes thinking through practical ways to help them regularly remember the Lord's faithfulness. "Train up a child in the way he should go," wrote King Solomon, "and when he is old he will not depart from it" (Proverbs 22:6).

Treat the things of God with reverence. The Lord commanded the people of Israel to cross the Jordan behind the ark of the covenant, but they were to keep a great distance back from it. This was a sign of deep respect for the ark, which symbolized God's presence with His people.

Their reverence served another purpose as well: the distance they kept from the ark enabled the entire nation to see it, and it drew the attention of the world around them to the ark rather than to the people. By remaining a thousand yards back, the people had no doubt that the power of God had parted the Jordan River, because the water divided the instant the priests' feet touched it.

This is actually a corollary to the previous principle. By holding the things of God in deep reverence, parents make it easier to teach their children to do the same. Parents draw their children's attention to the Lord and His commands by treating Him and His Word with respect, and this makes it easier for their children—and for their neighbors—to see the hand of God at work in their lives.

REFLECTING ON THE TEXT

5) What practical things do you and your family do to continually remember God's goodness and faithfulness? What things might you start doing in the future?

---

6) Why is it so important to teach children about the things of God? What happens if parents fail in that duty?

_____

_____

_____

_____

_____

7) Why did the Lord command the people to simply pile stones on top of one another rather than building an ornate shrine? What does this suggest about the focus of our own memorials?

_____

_____

_____

_____

_____

8) How is the Lord's Supper like the memorial the Israelites built? How does it differ? Why is it important to observe the Lord's Supper on a regular basis?

_____

_____

_____

_____

_____

PERSONAL RESPONSE

9) Do you treat the things of God with suitable reverence? What areas might the Lord be calling you to take more seriously?

_____

_____

_____

10) Are you faithful in teaching others about the things of God? What lessons do your children, neighbors, or coworkers learn from observing your life?

_____

_____

_____

3

THE FALL OF JERICHO
Joshua 5:1–6:27

DRAWING NEAR

The Israelites had to be persistent and march around Jericho for seven days before they saw the walls fall. How has persistence proven to be an asset in your life?

_____

_____

_____

THE CONTEXT

The people of Israel had crossed the Jordan River and were preparing to enter the land of Canaan, which the Lord had promised to give to the descendants of Abraham. However, as we have seen, there were many people already living in Canaan, and the region was peppered with several strong and fortified cities. Taking the land was going to involve warfare, and the Israelites would have to prepare themselves for battle.

Joshua had previously sent two spies into the well-fortified city of Jericho. In Joshua's day, the town was surrounded with massive walls made of mud brick and stone. These walls were often several feet thick, and many cities—including

Jericho—had two such walls, with a space between. The only way to enter such fortifications was through the main gate, and those gates were as strong and well guarded as the walls themselves.

Jericho was built on a tall mound of land and surrounded by an earthen embankment. It boasted a protection of two bulwarks, one inside the other. The outer wall was six feet thick, while the inner wall was twelve feet thick. Nothing is specifically known of its gate system, but it probably consisted of two gates, one in each wall, with a stone or brick tunnel connecting them. To attack the city, an enemy would have to charge uphill, climb over the embankment, and attempt to breach both gates—all while being shot at from above.

How were the Israelites to take such a city? They were not a trained army, and they had no high-tech weaponry at their disposal. What they did have, however, was more than enough: the presence of almighty God! As the people stood gazing on this powerful city, it must have become clear to them that the battle belonged to God, not to them.

KEYS TO THE TEXT

Read Joshua 5:1–6:27, noting the key words and phrases indicated below.

*REINSTATING THE COVENANT: As a final preparation for the
Israelites to enter into the Promised Land, God requires all the
young men in the camp to undergo circumcision.*

5:1. HEARD: The reports that God had supernaturally opened a crossing for the Israelites through the Jordan River struck fear into the Canaanites. The miracle was all the more incredible and shocking because God had performed it when the river was swollen to flood height. To the people in the land, this miracle—and the reports about the Red Sea miracle—proved that the God of the Israelites was indeed mighty.

5:2. CIRCUMCISE: God commanded Joshua to see this was done to all males under the age of forty. These were sons of the generation who died in the wilderness—survivors from the new generation that God spared in Numbers 13–14. The people had evidently ignored this surgical sign as a commitment of faith to the Abrahamic covenant during the wilderness trek. Now God wanted it reinstated so the Israelites would start out right in the land they were about to possess.

5:8. THEY WERE HEALED: This speaks of the time needed to recover from such a painful and potentially infected wound.

5:9. ROLLED AWAY THE REPROACH: By performing the miracle of bringing the people of Israel into the land, God removed (rolled away) the ridicule the Egyptians had heaped on them.

5:10. PASSOVER: This commemorated God's deliverance of the people from Egypt, as recorded in Exodus 7–12. Such a remembrance strengthened the people's resolve to trust in God as they took possession of the new land.

5:12. MANNA CEASED: God had provided this food from the time of Exodus 16 and did so for the next forty years (see Exodus 16:35). Because food was plentiful in the land of Canaan, the Israelites could now provide for themselves with produce such as dates, barley, and olives.

A VISIT FROM THE LORD: Joshua has a face-to-face encounter with God Himself. In many ways, this visit from God is similar to the calling of Moses at the burning bush.

13. JERICHO: See the map in the Introduction. Jericho was built atop a hill a few miles west of the Jordan River. Because of this, the city could only be taken by mounting a steep incline, which put the Israelites at a great disadvantage. Attackers of such a fortress often used a siege of several months to force surrender through starvation.

A MAN: This was the Lord Himself in a pre-incarnate appearance (called a *theophany*) as the Angel of the Lord. The naked sword in His hand indicated that He had come to exercise judgment—in this case, against Jericho.

14. AS COMMANDER OF THE ARMY OF THE LORD I HAVE NOW COME: The Lord was about to bring about a great victory for His people. However, this would not come through the military might of the Israelites but through "the army of the Lord." He would perform this great victory so that the glory would be His alone. Again, the Lord made it clear that this particular visit was for the purpose of judgment. (The Lord had once appeared to Abraham, as well, in like manner. He had visited Abraham at his tent, sharing His plans with him, as one friend to another.)

FELL ON HIS FACE TO THE EARTH: Joshua, though probably startled by the powerful and majestic appearance of the Man, did not realize exactly whom he was addressing. However, as soon as he realized that he was in the presence of the Lord, he threw himself facedown on the ground and worshiped. He also dramatically changed the tenor of his questions from "Whose side are you on?" to "How can I serve you?"

15. TAKE YOUR SANDAL OFF YOUR FOOT: This was an outward demonstration of humility and respect. Moses was given the same order to remove his shoes when the Lord called him into service as leader of His people. "Do not draw near this place. Take your sandals off your feet, for the place where you stand *is* holy ground" (Exodus 3:5).

CLOSED FOR THE DAY: The Israelites' presence in the land has created a panic among the people of Jericho, and they have shut themselves inside the walls of their city.

6:1. SECURELY SHUT UP: Many double-walled cities of that time had intricate, heavily fortified gate systems. Again, enemies could typically only defeat strong cities such as Jericho by cutting off the people's resources and waiting for the food and water to run out.

BECAUSE OF THE CHILDREN OF ISRAEL: The kings of the entire land, having heard how the Lord had dried up the Jordan River, were melting with fear—"there was no spirit in them any longer because of the children of Israel" (Joshua 5:1). Although the Lord had worked the great miracle of drying up the river primarily for the benefit of His people, He had also performed this wonder so the world would see and believe that He alone was the God of all creation.

2. I HAVE GIVEN JERICHO INTO YOUR HAND: The Lord repeatedly gave the Israelites complete victory over the cities of Canaan. The phrase generally indicated that the Israelites were to completely defeat their enemies, often without leaving any survivors.

3. MARCH AROUND THE CITY: The bizarre military strategy of marching around Jericho gave occasion for the Israelites to take God at His promise. The march would have also openly demonstrated to the residents of Jericho, as well as their neighbors, that the Israelites were holding the city captive. However, the Israelites' obvious lack of military action would have been extremely puzzling to observers. It was a public statement that the people of

Israel were depending on God, rather than their own military might, to deliver the city.

YOU SHALL GO ALL AROUND THE CITY ONCE: The city of Jericho occupied approximately seven acres of land, so the march around it would not have taken very long.

4. TRUMPETS OF RAMS' HORNS: Rams' horns were used in combat as well as in religious exercises to gather the people together. The ark of the covenant went with the people in their march around the walls, indicating to the entire world that it was the Lord Himself who was leading Israel.

THE SEVENTH DAY YOU SHALL MARCH AROUND THE CITY SEVEN TIMES: The number seven in Scripture often represents completion. For example, the Lord created the entire universe in six days, then rested on the seventh day (Genesis 2:1–3).

THE WALL OF THE CITY WILL FALL: God assured Israel of an astounding miracle, just as He had done at the Jordan River.

5. ALL THE PEOPLE SHALL SHOUT: The Lord's command for the people to shout is noteworthy, because it indicated that a great triumph was about to be wrought. At the end of earth's history, "The Lord Himself will descend from heaven with a shout, with the voice of an archangel, and with the trumpet of God" (1 Thessalonians 4:16).

10. OR MAKE ANY NOISE WITH YOUR VOICE: This was similar to the command for the people to stay back from the ark as they crossed the Jordan River. It was a sign of meekness and reverence in the presence of the Lord, and it also provided the people a chance to meditate quietly on the character of God as they marched around the walls. It also must have been extremely disconcerting to the people inside those walls to watch the silent procession.

THE WALLS COME TUMBLING DOWN: The people of Israel follow the Lord's instructions exactly, and He works a powerful miracle on their behalf.

17. DOOMED BY THE LORD TO DESTRUCTION: The Hebrew term for *doomed* means "utterly destroyed." In this, we see that the Lord had literally devoted to ruin the entire city of Jericho. This concept is found frequently in the book of Joshua and elsewhere in the Old Testament, and it referred to consecrating something (such as pottery and other objects) to complete destruction

as a sacrifice to the Lord. Cities such as Jericho had sunk themselves so deeply into wickedness that the Lord demanded their absolute obliteration—not only their material possessions but every living thing as well.

RAHAB THE HARLOT: As we have seen, Rahab entered the book of Joshua as a harlot, but she would finish her life for the Lord. The two spies Joshua had sent to investigate Jericho had promised Rahab that she and her family would be kept safe if they aided them in their mission, and Joshua accepted their promise as binding. God's children are to be people of their word.

18. ABSTAIN FROM THE ACCURSED THINGS: The people of Jericho had become so wicked in the Lord's sight that even their possessions were corrupted, and God was determined for His people to keep themselves pure from such contamination. Joshua warned the people in strong terms: "by all means" they should keep themselves away from the "things" of Jericho.

LEST YOU BECOME ACCURSED WHEN YOU TAKE OF THE ACCURSED THINGS: To associate in any way with those whom God had placed under judgment—even to the point of taking away loot from their destruction—was to make oneself accursed along with those whom God had cursed. This stern warning was well warranted, as we will see when we look at the sin of Achan.

20. THE WALL FELL DOWN FLAT: Archaeological studies have found that the city of Jericho probably existed during a time of several earthquakes. It is possible that the Lord used such natural forces to bring down the city's walls, and perhaps also to dam up the Jordan River. But if such natural disasters were used, they were still not the cause of Jericho's miraculous devastation. It was the Lord Himself who brought down the walls, and whatever means He may have used to accomplish the miracle do not lessen His sovereignty.

22. AS YOU SWORE TO HER: Once again, Joshua took great care to ensure that he kept his word to Rahab—even though he had not given his word directly.

23. BROUGHT OUT RAHAB: The part of the wall securing Rahab's house must not have fallen, and all possessions in the dwelling were safe.

26. CURSED BE THE MAN: God put a curse on whoever would rebuild Jericho. While the area around it was later occupied to some extent, the curse came to pass many centuries later when a man named Hiel attempted to rebuild the city's walls and gates at the cost of his sons' lives (see 1 Kings 16:34).

27. THE LORD WAS WITH JOSHUA: God kept His pledge to be with Joshua: "As I was with Moses, so I will be with you. I will not leave you nor forsake you" (Joshua 1:5).

UNLEASHING THE TEXT

1) If you had been with the Israelites, how would you have felt about marching around Jericho every day?

_____

_____

_____

2) If you had been inside the city of Jericho, how would you have felt as you watched the Israelites marching each day?

_____

_____

_____

_____

3) Why did the people of Jericho lock themselves inside the city? Why did they not charge out and attack the Israelites?

_____

_____

_____

4) Why did the Lord instruct the people to carry the ark with them? Why did they blow rams' horns? Why were they not permitted to speak?

_____

_____

_____

EXPLORING THE MEANING

Obey the Lord's commands, even if they don't address your immediate concerns. Joshua and the Israelites were immediately concerned with the city of Jericho. It was a powerfully fortified city that lay directly in their path into Canaan, and they could not afford to leave it standing at their back as they entered the Promised Land. They needed to conquer that great city—but the Lord commanded them to spend a week marching around it, blowing horns. This must have seemed a strange command at the time.

Yet the Lord had His own plans for Jericho, and He wanted the people of Israel and the world around to see conclusively that He was the one who would knock down its walls. His command to march around the wall was not frivolous, even though the people of Israel probably did not see the full meaning of it at the time. Their job was just to obey, not to try to comprehend the mind of God.

The Lord's commands frequently go directly against what the world teaches, and there can be times when God's people will not see the full reason for obeying His Word. After all, the Bible was written thousands of years ago, and it is easy to fall into the trap of assuming its commands and precepts are not relevant today. But the Lord's Word stands for all time, and His commands are as relevant to us today as they were when they were first penned. It may not be evident how obedience to God's Word will resolve a difficult situation, but our job is to obey what the Bible teaches and trust the Lord to take care of our circumstances.

Let the Lord fight the battles. God commanded the Israelites to enter the land of Canaan and subdue it. This frequently involved warfare, and God's people needed to learn how to fight. But it was important for them to remember the battle was the Lord's, not theirs, whether their part involved taking up arms or merely marching around a city's walls and blowing rams' horns.

The Christian's warfare is mostly of a spiritual nature, as we are called to fight against spiritual forces rather than against other people. It is easy sometimes to lose sight of this fact, however, as our lives are frequently affected by the actions of people around us. The Lord wants His people to live responsibly, and we should take whatever actions we can within His will. But the battles we face are the Lord's, whether or not there is anything we can do on a human level. He wants us to place our faith in His sovereignty and remember that the outcome of our lives is entirely in His hands.

Hear these words from Deuteronomy: "The LORD your God, who goes before you, He will fight for you, according to all He did for you in Egypt before your eyes, and in the wilderness where you saw how the LORD your God carried you, as a man carries his son, in all the way that you went until you came to this place" (1:30–31).

God's people are to keep themselves pure from the world's pollution. The Lord had condemned the entire city of Jericho because of the wickedness of its people, and His condemnation extended even to the citizens' possessions and livestock. Everything had to be destroyed, because it was all tainted with corruption. God also commanded His people to refrain from keeping any plunder, lest they too be led into wickedness through the idols and other evil things they might find.

This principle is important in our lives as modern Christians because we are not a separate nation—we live in the world and must interact with it in some measure. Yet the Lord called His people to be *in* the world, not *of* it (see John 15:19), and we are not to partake in the sinful nature of the world's system. To stand guard against impurity requires constant diligence, lest we gradually come to love the things of the world and lose sight of our calling to holiness.

"Do not love the world," wrote the apostle John, "or the things in the world. If anyone loves the world, the love of the Father is not in him. For all that is in the world—the lust of the flesh, the lust of the eyes, and the pride of life—is not of the Father but is of the world. And the world is passing away, and the lust of it; but he who does the will of God abides forever" (1 John 2:15–17).

REFLECTING ON THE TEXT

5) Why did the Lord conquer Jericho the way He did? Why did He not have the Israelites attack outright?

_____

_____

_____

6) Why did the Lord command the Israelites to completely destroy the city, including the people's possessions? Why were the Israelites not to take any of the spoils?

_____

_____

_____

7) In what ways does the world sometimes lead Christians into corruption? Give specific examples.

_____

_____

_____

8) What steps should Christians take to avoid being corrupted by the world?

_____

_____

_____

PERSONAL RESPONSE

9) What battles in your life have you been trying to fight for yourself? How can you leave those battles in the Lord's hands this week?

_____

_____

_____

10) Are there areas in your life that have become corrupted by the world's
    values? What must you do to purify those areas?

_____

_____

_____

4

THE SIN OF ACHAN

Joshua 7:1–8:35

DRAWING NEAR

What does it mean to "covet" something? What are some of the common
things that people covet in our world today?

_____

_____

_____

THE CONTEXT

God had just given Joshua and the Israelites an incredible victory at the city
of Jericho. The people had marched around the city seven times, the priests
had blown the trumpets, and the walls had fallen down. However, as part of
that victory, God had instructed the Israelites to not take anything whatsoever
away from Jericho after its fall. Everything was to be destroyed as a sacrifice to
God. The Lord had claimed the entire city of Jericho for Himself, and it was to
be dedicated to Him and utterly set apart from the people.

But, as we will see in this study, one man decided to disregard God's command. Perhaps he had convinced himself that God was speaking in broad, general terms—that He would not mind or even notice if one man took just a few

small trinkets. Or perhaps he didn't think at all; maybe he just snatched what he saw without giving any thought to the possible consequences. Whatever he may have told himself, this man named Achan fell prey to the sin of coveting, and it led to deadly consequences for his entire family.

In this study, we will look at Achan's story and consider the dangers of coveting. We will also see that we cannot hide anything from God, for He sees both what we do and what we think. This can be a sobering concept for us if we try to hide our sins from God, but it can also be a great deterrent from sin and temptation.

Keys to the Text

Read Joshua 7:1–8:35, noting the key words and phrases indicated below.

PREPARING FOR BATTLE: *Joshua prepares his army to attack Ai soon after the battle against Jericho. What he doesn't know, however, is that there is sin in the camp.*

7:1. THE ACCURSED THINGS: The Lord had commanded the people to "abstain from the accursed things, lest you become accursed when you take of the accursed things, and make the camp of Israel a curse, and trouble it" (Joshua 6:18). God had condemned all of Jericho—all its inhabitants and all their possessions—to destruction, and the people were forbidden to carry away anything whatsoever. Achan, however, had taken a souvenir.

2. AI: See the map in the Introduction.

3. LET ABOUT TWO OR THREE THOUSAND MEN GO UP: This proved to be a gross strategic error and miscalculation. The spies thought there were "few" inhabitants in Ai, but it turned out there were some twelve thousand people there (see Joshua 8:25)—far too many for a small force of three thousand to take, at least from a human perspective. The spies may have anticipated the Lord would fight on their behalf, as He had done at Jericho and elsewhere. If so, their faith was commendable, and it would certainly be justified later when the Lord did bring down Ai. However, in this case there is no record that Joshua consulted the Lord prior to making his strategic plans. If he had, the Lord would certainly have told him to not attack at that time—there was sin in the camp that needed to be dealt with first.

ISRAEL'S FIRST DEFEAT: As a result of Achan's sin, the Lord does not fight on behalf of His people. They find out what it is like to have God set His face against them.

5. THE HEARTS OF THE PEOPLE MELTED: This is the phrase Rahab used to describe the dismay the people of Jericho had felt toward Israel. Because of Achan's sin, the Lord had removed His protective hand from His people, and they were experiencing the same dismay to which God's enemies were subject.

6. JOSHUA . . . FELL TO THE EARTH ON HIS FACE BEFORE THE ARK OF THE LORD: Joshua's failure is that he had not sought the Lord's counsel before attacking Ai. He should have come to God and humbly sought His guidance before moving ahead.

9. WHAT WILL YOU DO FOR YOUR GREAT NAME: Joshua's concern in his prayer is twofold: he is concerned for the welfare of the people for whom he is responsible, and he is worried the Lord's name will be disgraced.

11. ISRAEL HAS SINNED: It is important to note the Lord held the *entire* nation responsible for the sin of one man. Achan had hidden his sin, and it is unlikely Joshua knew of it—yet Achan's family knew, and they had assisted him simply by keeping his secret. Thus, the sin of Achan had corrupted the entire assembly of God's people and was directly responsible for Israel's military defeat and the deaths of thirty-six soldiers.

12. THEY HAVE BECOME DOOMED TO DESTRUCTION: By taking an object that God had doomed to destruction, the people themselves had also become doomed to destruction. The consequences of sin often go far beyond just the person sinning and affect the lives of others. Such is the destructive power of disobedience.

PURGING THE EVIL: The Lord commands Joshua to find the guilty man and put him to death. The penalty extends to his family and all his possessions.

15. BURNED WITH FIRE: This sounds like a harsh punishment for such a "small" sin as looting a city that the Israelite army had defeated in battle. But man's view of sin is often not harsh enough, for God detests sin and will not tolerate it in His presence. Furthermore, the Lord had warned that everything associated with Jericho was to be set aside for destruction, and

anyone who took anything from the city would bring destruction upon himself. Achan knew this beforehand but had deluded himself into thinking he could deceive God.

19. GIVE GLORY TO THE LORD: Achan had tried to hide his sin, and in doing so he had brought disgrace on the Lord's name. By openly admitting his sin, he would be glorifying God, acknowledging that he was guilty of breaking God's holy standard.

21. I SAW: Note the four steps in Achan's sin: (1) he *saw,* (2) he *coveted,* (3) he *took,* and (4) he *concealed.* David's sin with Bathsheba would follow the same pattern (see 2 Samuel 11). James tells us, "Each one is tempted when he is drawn away by his own desires and enticed. Then, when desire has conceived, it gives birth to sin." But never forget the consequence: "Sin, when it is full-grown, brings forth death" (James 1:14–15).

A BEAUTIFUL BABYLONIAN GARMENT: This was a costly and ornate robe of Shinar. It would have been adorned with colored figures of men or animals, woven or done in needlework, and perhaps trimmed with jewels. This same word is used for a king's robe in Jonah 3:6.

24. ALL THAT HE HAD: Once again, we are confronted with the fact that the sin of one man brought destruction on many. His entire family was implicated because they each had assisted him in concealing the sin. The Lord viewed that action as being complicit in the sin itself.

26. VALLEY OF ACHOR: Literally "trouble."

RESETTING THE SCENE: Now that Joshua has dealt with the sin in the Israelite camp, the Lord will deliver the king of Ai into his hand.

8:3. THIRTY THOUSAND . . . MEN: Joshua's elite force was far superior to that of Ai, which, as we mentioned, had an army of twelve thousand. This time Joshua took no small force into the battle but thirty thousand mighty men of valor. He used some of this force to sack and burn Ai, a decoy group to lure defenders out of the city, and a third detachment of about five thousand men to prevent the nearby city of Bethel from helping Ai.

7. GOD WILL DELIVER IT INTO YOUR HAND: God had sovereignly caused Israel's defeat earlier due to Achan's disobedience. This time, despite Israel's overwhelming numbers, God would still be the sovereign power behind the victory.

18. THE SPEAR: Joshua's hoisted javelin represented the go-ahead indicator for the troops to occupy Ai. The raised weapon was possibly even a signal of Joshua's confidence that God would deliver the city into his hand. Earlier, Moses' uplifted rod and arms likely signified a similar trust in God for victory over the Amalekites (see Exodus 17:8–13).

29. THE KING OF AI: The execution of Ai's populace included hanging the king. This wise move would have prevented later efforts to muster a Canaanite army. Further, as a wicked king, he was worthy of punishment according to biblical standards. This carried out the vengeance of God on His enemies.

30. JOSHUA BUILT AN ALTAR . . . AS MOSES THE SERVANT OF THE LORD HAD COMMANDED: This ceremony took place in obedience to Deuteronomy 27:1–26 at the conclusion of Joshua's central campaign.

31. AN ALTAR OF WHOLE STONES: In obedience to the instruction of Exodus 20:24–26, Joshua built the altar of uncut stones, thus keeping the worship simple and untainted by human showmanship. Joshua gave God's Word a detailed and central place.

GOING DEEPER

Read 1 Timothy 6:6–10, 17–19, noting the key words and phrases below.

INSTRUCTIONS REGARDING MONEY AND POSSESSIONS: Paul warns Timothy against the sin of greed that Achan had committed at Jericho.

6:6. GODLINESS WITH CONTENTMENT: This Greek word translated *contentment* refers to self-sufficiency. Stoic philosophers used the term to describe a person who was unflappable and unmoved by external circumstances. Christians are to be satisfied, sufficient, and not to seek more than what God has already given them. The Lord is the source of true contentment.

8. HAVING FOOD AND CLOTHING . . . BE CONTENT: As Christians, we should be content with the basic necessities of life. Paul does not condemn us for having possessions, as long as God graciously provides them. He does, however, condemn a self-indulgent desire for money, which results from discontentment. "But seek first the kingdom of God and His righteousness, and all these things shall be added to you" (Matthew 6:33).

9. THOSE WHO DESIRE TO BE RICH FALL INTO TEMPTATION: *Desire* refers to a settled wish that is born of reason and clearly describes those guilty of greed. The form of the Greek verb for *fall* indicates that those who have such a desire are continually falling into temptation. Greedy people are compulsive—they are continually trapped in sin by their consuming desire to acquire more.

DESTRUCTION AND PERDITION: Such greed may lead these people to suffer the tragic end of destruction and hell. These terms refer to the eternal punishment of the wicked.

10. LOVE OF MONEY: Literally "affection for silver." Paul does not condemn money itself as being evil, for it is a gift from God (see Deuteronomy 8:18), but he does condemn the love of it.

17. COMMAND THOSE WHO ARE RICH: Paul here counsels Timothy on what to teach those who are rich in material possessions—those who have more than the mere essentials of food, clothing, and shelter. Once again, Paul does not condemn such people, nor does he command them to get rid of their wealth, but he does call them to be good stewards of the God-given resources they have received.

17. NOT TO BE HAUGHTY: *Haughty* means "to have an exalted opinion of oneself." Those who have an abundance are constantly tempted to look down on others and act superior to them. Riches and pride often go together. The wealthier a person is, the more he is tempted to be proud (see Proverbs 18:23; 28:11; James 2:1–4).

UNCERTAIN RICHES . . . GIVES US RICHLY: Those who have much tend to trust in their wealth, but God provides far more security than any earthly investment can ever give.

18. READY TO GIVE: The Greek word means "liberal" or "bountiful." Believers who have money must use it unselfishly and generously to meet the needs of others.

19. STORING UP . . . A GOOD FOUNDATION: *Storing up* can be translated "amassing a treasure," while *foundation* can refer to a fund. The idea is that the rich in this world should not be concerned with receiving a return on their earthly investment. Those who make eternal investments will be content to receive their dividends in heaven.

UNLEASHING THE TEXT

1) Why did the Lord command the Israelites to not take anything from Jericho?

_____

_____

_____

2) Why did Achan disobey the Lord's command? What motivated him?

_____

_____

_____

3) What was Joshua's main concern when Israel lost the battle against Ai? How did his attitude compare with Achan's?

_____

_____

_____

4) Why did Achan bury the loot under his tent? What did this reveal about his attitude toward God?

_____

_____

_____

Exploring the Meaning

The things of the world can bring corruption. At the time the Israelites defeated Jericho, it was customary for a victorious army to plunder the defeated foe. From the perspective of war, Achan was well within his rights to take a few things after the battle. The items he came away with were not evil in themselves—a beautiful garment, some cash, and a wedge of gold. The problem was the Lord had clearly commanded His people to not take away *any* loot from Jericho. Interestingly, the Lord did permit them to carry away possessions from Ai. If Achan had simply obeyed at Jericho, he would have been more than compensated in the next battle.

The Lord frequently calls His people to refrain from worldly habits and pursuits—to obey His Word even when worldly pleasures tug our hearts in a different direction. The lust of the flesh, the lust of the eyes, and the boastful pride of life continually tempt us to sin. Like Achan, our hearts can be enticed by feelings of covetousness, greed, envy, and the desires of our flesh. The question is whether or not we will resist the temptation and be obedient to the Lord.

The principle here is that the Lord calls His people to be set apart from the world—and this frequently includes avoiding contact with worldly activities. "For you are the temple of the living God. As God has said: 'I will dwell in them and walk among them. I will be their God, and they shall be my people.' Therefore 'Come out from among them and be separate, says the Lord. Do not touch what is unclean, and I will receive you'" (2 Corinthians 6:16–17).

God cannot be deceived. Achan understood the Lord's command not to touch any of the treasures in Jericho, but he believed he could take just a few small items without any consequences. He then buried those items in the ground beneath his tent—an excellent hiding place if ever there was one. Achan and his family believed they could hide their sin from God.

The fact is that they did succeed in hiding their sin from other people. It would appear that nobody outside of Achan's family was aware of the stolen property, and Joshua confidently led the army into battle in the belief that all was well. Yet the Lord knew what Achan had done, and He was not willing to overlook the transgression. All sin, no matter how small in the world's eyes, is an abhorrent offense in the eyes of God.

It is easy to hide our sins from the people around us, but we can never hide our transgressions from God. He calls His people to purify their lives from all sins and confess them openly before Him. "Do not be deceived, God is not mocked; for whatever a man sows, that he will also reap. For he who sows to his flesh will of the flesh reap corruption, but he who sows to the Spirit will of the Spirit reap everlasting life" (Galatians 6:7–8).

Covetousness is the same as idolatry. Achan was motivated by covetousness. He confessed it was his own eyes that had led him into sin: he *saw* beautiful things in Jericho and *coveted* them in his heart. What he coveted, he also took . . . and what he took, he finally hid.

It is not a sin to admire beautiful things, but it is a sin to *covet*. To covet is to lust for something—to fix one's mind on material possessions or financial gain. We begin to covet when we long to possess something that does not belong to us and when we become absorbed with getting what we don't have. Achan did not sin when he noticed that the garment in Jericho was lovely. He sinned when he determined he had to own it in spite of God's prohibition.

When we covet, we fix our hearts on material goods, and those desires begin to drive our thoughts, actions, and attitudes. In this way, the thing we covet becomes like a god to us—an "idol" in our lives. The Lord wants us to fix our eyes on Him alone, turning them away from the goods of this world. "Put to death . . . covetousness, which is idolatry" (Colossians 3:5).

REFLECTING ON THE TEXT

5) What steps did Achan take in his sin? When have you taken similar steps that led to sin?

_____

_____

_____

_____

6) Why did God command Achan's entire family to be put to death? What does this severe punishment reveal about God's view of disobedience?

_____

_____

_____

7) What exactly is covetousness? How is coveting an object different from admiring it? How can we tell the difference?

_____

_____

_____

8) In what ways is covetousness the same as idolatry? How can we recognize it in our lives?

_____

_____

_____

Personal Response

9) Are you struggling with covetousness? What do you covet? What biblical principles and practical steps can you apply in your life to overcome this temptation?

_____

_____

_____

10) Are you trying to hide any sins from God? If so, take time right now to confess them to the Lord. He is faithful and just to forgive (see 1 John 1:9).

_____

_____

_____

5

THE SUN STANDS STILL
Joshua 9:1–10:25

DRAWING NEAR

Why do you think some people find it difficult to believe the miracles in the Bible? How have you seen people try to explain these events away as other than the miraculous hand of God?

_____

_____

_____

THE CONTEXT

The Lord had now led Joshua and the Israelites to great victories over Jericho and Ai, and word had spread throughout Canaan that Israel's God was fighting on their behalf. The people of Canaan were filled with terror, for they realized they could not possibly stand against the wrath of the almighty God. Most of the cities of Canaan responded to this threat by aggressively attacking Israel in hopes of defeating her armies before the Lord could intervene. One city, however, adopted a different approach.

The city of Gibeon was located northwest of Jerusalem and about seven miles from Ai. The people of this town wisely determined to make peace with the Israelites, as they recognized they could not win if they remained enemies. However, instead of asking for peace directly, they resorted to subterfuge by pretending they lived far away and posed no threat to God's people. The leaders of Israel were deceived by this ruse and signed a covenant in God's name to live at peace with Gibeon.

Meanwhile, the king of Jerusalem formed an alliance with four other kings, and they desperately sought a way to defeat Israel. When they learned of Gibeon's peace covenant, they realized their best course was to attack Israel's friends rather than Israel itself. God honored Israel's covenant with Gibeon, and He would not allow the Canaanite kings to defeat that city any more than He would permit His own people to be destroyed.

So the Lord commanded Joshua to attack the five kings and their armies. Israel's armies were probably outnumbered, and they arrived at the scene of battle already exhausted from an all-night uphill march. However, the Lord Himself intended to fight the battle, so it didn't matter what the odds were against Israel. God showed Himself faithful and omnipotent that day, proving there was nothing He could not or would not do for the sake of His people— even to the point of moving heaven and earth on Israel's behalf.

KEYS TO THE TEXT

Read Joshua 9:1–10:25, noting the key words and phrases indicated below.

> THE GIBEONITE RUSE: *The people of Canaan are now filled with fear as the Israelites approach. One town decides to meet this threat by deceiving the Israelites into making a peace treaty.*

9:3. WHEN THE INHABITANTS OF GIBEON: Gibeon of the Hivites or Horites was a strong city with capable fighting men (see Joshua 10:2). Three other towns were in league with it: Chephirah, Beeroth, and Kirjath Jearim (see 9:17).

4. PRETENDED TO BE AMBASSADORS: The Gibeonite delegation dressed in old clothes and used worn-out provisions to make it appear as if they had traveled from a distant land.

14. THEY DID NOT ASK COUNSEL OF THE LORD: The Gibeonite plot worked because the Israelites were not vigilant in prayer to assure that they acted by God's counsel.

15. JOSHUA MADE PEACE WITH THEM: Because of this failure, Israel precipitously made peace with the Gibeonites who lived nearby, even though God had instructed them to eliminate the people of the cities in the land (see Deuteronomy 7:1–2). God had permitted them to make peace with cities outside Canaan (see Deuteronomy 20:11–15).

19. WE MAY NOT TOUCH THEM: The rulers of Israel soon discovered the deception, but there was nothing they could do to undo the terms of the covenant. This would quickly come back to trouble them when the king of Jerusalem used this peace agreement to his advantage.

23. YOU ARE CURSED: Joshua honored the pledge of peace with the Gibeonites but made them woodcutters and water carriers because of the deception. Gibeon became a part of Benjamin's land area (see Joshua 18:25). Later, Joshua would consign Gibeon as one of the Levite towns (see 21:17), and Nehemiah would receive help from some Gibeonites in rebuilding the walls of Jerusalem (see Nehemiah 3:7).

THE LEAGUE AGAINST ISRAEL: *Other cities in Canaan decide to meet the rising threat of the Israelites by banding together to confront them as a combined military force.*

10:1. JERUSALEM: In the time of Joshua, this important city may have been called Salem rather than Jerusalem. It was an important city in Abraham's day as well, when Melchizedek was its king. In Genesis 14, we read that Melchizedek came out and met Abraham as he returned from rescuing his nephew Lot. In fact, this king (and by virtue of his position, his kingdom) blessed Abraham. The city's attitude toward Abraham's descendants, however, was vastly different. The Lord had promised to bless those who blessed Israel and curse those who cursed Israel. Now that the people of Salem were setting themselves against Israel, their days were numbered.

GIBEON HAD MADE PEACE WITH ISRAEL: As previously discussed, the people of Gibeon used deception to make peace with Israel rather than straightforward surrender.

2. THEY FEARED GREATLY: The people of Jerusalem were wise to fear the power of Israel, because its might came directly from God, and He was tearing down those cities that had devoted themselves to pagan gods. Still, Jerusalem's people deluded themselves with the belief that they could defeat the power of

God by forming an alliance with their neighbors. Gibeon's inhabitants showed themselves to be wiser by humbling themselves and seeking peace.

3. HEBRON . . . JARMUTH . . . LACHISH . . . EGLON: See the map in the Introduction.

DO NOT BE AFRAID: *The Canaanite kings are afraid to attack Israel, so they do the next best thing: they attack Israel's allies. However, the Lord tells Joshua not to fear them, for He will fight Israel's battles and give them great victory.*

4. THAT WE MAY ATTACK GIBEON: Those who make peace with God, or even with God's people, open themselves to the attack of God's enemies. The Canaanite kings may have recognized they could not defeat Israel in direct combat, but they evidently thought they could discourage other cities from making peace.

6. DO NOT FORSAKE YOUR SERVANTS: The people of Israel had made a mistake when they formed a covenant with the inhabitants of Gibeon. Nevertheless, the Lord honored that covenant and protected the people of Gibeon in spite of this treacherous deception.

8. DO NOT FEAR THEM: It is significant the Lord gives this as a command to Joshua, rather than mere words of encouragement, such as "cheer up." The Lord *commands* His people to resist fear and choose to deliberately stand strong in courage. Ultimately, our courage is drawn from the character of God: we choose to place our faith in Him because we know He is faithful. Giving in to fear, therefore, is a lack of faith in God's character. Fear is what motivated the people of Jerusalem and other Canaanite cities—they had no faith in the God of Israel and therefore fell prey to their own terror.

9. HAVING MARCHED ALL NIGHT FROM GILGAL: Gilgal was approximately twenty miles from Gibeon, and the march was mostly uphill.

10. THE LORD ROUTED THEM: The word translated *routed* implies that the enemy was thrown into great confusion and panic. The Israelites' victory was all the more dramatic because they had just been through an all-night march uphill, carrying their weapons and gear. They would have been fatigued prior to the fight, but the Lord fought the battle on their behalf. When we place our trust in God and stand firm against fear, the Lord always proves Himself faithful. This is the key to being victorious in the Christian life.

TWO GREAT MIRACLES: God sends great hailstones on the enemy and then He causes the sun to stand still in the sky.

11. THE LORD CAST DOWN LARGE HAILSTONES FROM HEAVEN: The hailstones provide direct evidence that this battle was being fought by the Lord, not by Israel's military might. They selectively fell only on the enemy "as far as Azekah," and they killed more than those who fell by the sword. Joshua and his army needed to be present during the battle, as the Lord had commanded them to fight, but the ultimate victory would not be won through their military prowess.

13. THE SUN STOOD STILL: Many scholars have attempted to explain away what occurred on this day, suggesting there was an eclipse of the sun, or that the author was only speaking poetically rather than literally. Yet there is no question the author (probably Joshua himself) was literally recounting a historical event. The only plausible explanation, therefore, is that the Lord miraculously caused the earth to pause in its rotation and the moon to briefly halt in its orbit. This is one of the most dramatic miracles in the Old Testament— and yet it pales in comparison with the miracles of the New Testament, where God Himself became a man, born of a virgin; where God the Son resurrected those who were dead; where God the Father resurrected His Son from the dead; and where the resurrected Son offered salvation to those who had no hope and who were already dead in their sins. Those who have placed their faith in the salvation plan of Christ should have no trouble placing their faith in a miracle that is simple by comparison, such as the sun standing still—or any other marvel the Lord performs.

BOOK OF JASHER: Jasher means *upright.* The book appears to have been a compilation of Hebrew songs in honor of Israel's leaders and exploits in battle, and it may have been the same as the book called *Wars of the Lord* (see Numbers 21:14). The Book of Jasher is mentioned again in 2 Samuel 1:18, and a portion of it is recorded in 1:19–27.

24. FEET ON THE NECKS: This gesture symbolized the Israelites' victory and promised assurance of future conquest.

25. BE STRONG AND OF GOOD COURAGE: Here again we find the command to resist fear and be of good courage. We tend to think of fear as an emotion, a reflexive response over which we have no control, but that is not what the Scriptures teach. Again, we are *commanded* to be strong and fill our hearts

and minds with courage, even when we are faced with circumstances that urge us to be afraid. Courage is a deliberate choice, not an instinctive response or some innate ability some people have and others do not. All God's people are charged to choose strength and courage instead of fear and weakness. This is accomplished by deliberately electing to place our faith in God's sovereignty and faithfulness. He defeated the enemies of Israel in the past, and He will defeat the enemies of His people in the future.

GOING DEEPER

Read 2 Timothy 1:6–12, noting the key words and phrases below.

FEAR NOT: Paul provides additional instruction on how Christians are to overcome fear and lead a victorious life.

1:6. STIR UP THE GIFT OF GOD: *Stir up* means literally "to keep the fire alive," and *gift* refers to the believer's spiritual gift. Paul reminds Timothy that as a steward of his God-given gift for preaching, teaching, and evangelizing, he could not let it fall into disuse.

7. A SPIRIT OF FEAR: The Greek word for *fear*, which can also be translated "timidity," denotes a cowardly fear caused by a weak and selfish character. The threat of Roman persecution, the hostility of those in the Ephesian church who resented Timothy's leadership, and the assaults of false teachers with their sophisticated systems of deception may have been overwhelming Timothy. But if he was fearful, it didn't come from God.

BUT OF POWER: God has given believers all the spiritual resources they need for every trial and threat. Divine power—effective, productive spiritual energy—belongs to believers.

AND OF LOVE: This kind of love centers on pleasing God and seeking others' welfare before one's own.

AND OF A SOUND MIND: This refers to a disciplined, self-controlled, and properly prioritized mind. This is the opposite of fear and cowardice that causes disorder and confusion. Focusing on the sovereign nature and perfect purposes of our eternal God allows believers to control their lives with godly wisdom and confidence in every situation.

8. THE TESTIMONY OF OUR LORD: Paul did not want Timothy to be "ashamed" to proclaim the name of Christ because he was afraid of the potential persecution.

ME HIS PRISONER: At the time Paul wrote this letter, he was in jail for preaching the gospel. His link to Timothy could have put the younger man's life and freedom in jeopardy.

9. WITH A HOLY CALLING: Paul asks Timothy to share with him in suffering for the sake of the gospel and to remember his holy calling. This calling is not a general invitation to sinners to believe the gospel and be saved (as in Matthew 20:16), but instead it refers to God's effectual call of the elect to salvation. This calling results in holiness, imputed (justification) and imparted (sanctification), and finally completed (glorification).

10. ABOLISHED DEATH AND BROUGHT LIFE: *Abolished* means "rendered inoperative." Physical death still exists, but it is no longer a threat or an enemy that Christians need to fear. It was not until the incarnation and the gospel that God chose to make known fully the truth of immortality and eternal life—a reality only partially understood by Joshua and the other Old Testament believers.

12. I AM NOT ASHAMED: Paul had no fear of persecution and death from preaching the gospel in a hostile setting because he was so confident God had sealed his future glory and blessing. Paul lived with unwavering confidence and boldness because of the truth that had been revealed to him about God's power and faithfulness and his own experience of an unbreakable relationship with the Lord.

UNLEASHING THE TEXT

1) Why did the Canaanite kings attack Gibeon rather than Israel? What principle does this illustrate concerning the world's attitude toward God's people?

_____

_____

_____

2) Why did God use hailstones to defeat the Canaanite armies? Why not just allow Joshua's army to win the battle outright?

_____

_____

_____

3) Why did Joshua command the sun to stand still? What did this reveal about his faith?

_____

_____

_____

4) Why did God honor Joshua's bold command? What does this reveal about His character?

_____

_____

_____

Exploring the Meaning

God can literally move heaven and earth to accomplish His purposes. Or, to speak more specifically to the events discussed in this chapter, the Lord can cause the earth and heavens (the atmosphere) to *not* move. In order for the sun to "stand still," the earth would have needed to stop revolving on its axis—and evidently this is exactly what the Lord did for the Israelites on that momentous day. He literally caused the earth to stop for a period of hours so His people would have victory in battle.

The Lord went beyond even this "earthshaking" miracle when He moved heaven itself—the abode of God—to send His Son to earth as a man. He temporarily set aside the laws of biology and caused a virgin to become pregnant with the Son of God. More than this, He permitted His Holy One to take on the sin of mankind, caused the One who is Life to taste death, and subjected the Creator to the whims of those He had created. He did all of this so we might be reconciled with Him.

If God would do all of this for the sake of sinful people, He will certainly prove faithful in meeting our present needs. Some problems may be too great for us to resolve in our own power, but there is no problem too great for God.

Do not be afraid, but be strong and of good courage. This commandment appears frequently in the book of Joshua—usually at times when there seems to be genuine cause for fear. For instance, in Joshua 10 the army of Israel had marched all night long, uphill, carrying their battle gear. They had arrived to face not one but five enemy armies, and they were tired before the battle even began. Yet the Lord commanded His people to not give in to fear. "For God has not given us a spirit of fear, but of power and of love and of a sound mind" (2 Timothy 1:7).

Fear is the enemy of God's people because it moves them away from faith and toward disobedience. For example, when the people of Israel first arrived at the Jordan River to take possession of the Promised Land, their spies had brought back a discouraging report. There were giants in the land and fortified cities, and the reports made the people afraid. The Israelites yielded to that fear and disobeyed the Lord, dooming that entire generation to die in the wilderness (see Numbers 13–14).

We are commanded to resist fear, which demonstrates that fear is something we can master. This is done by shifting our focus away from the situation that threatens us and focusing on the Lord who redeems us. He is absolutely sovereign over all our affairs, and He is completely faithful to save His people. If He was willing to make the sun stand still for Israel's army, He will be willing to intervene in our lives as well.

God blesses those who bless Israel. All the people of Canaan were filled with terror at the approach of Israel because they knew what the Lord had done on their behalf at Jericho. Most of those cities, with the exception of Gibeon, responded by waging war against God's people. The Gibeonites' methods were more perverse—they used trickery to deceive Joshua into making a covenant of peace. In spite of this ruse, the Lord honored that covenant and allowed the Gibeonites to remain in Canaan.

This principle goes back to the time of Abraham. God promised Abraham (then called Abram), "I will bless those who bless you, and I will curse him who curses you; and in you all the families of the earth shall be blessed" (Genesis 12:3). The Lord proved Himself faithful to that promise again and again throughout the Old Testament, and the promise is still in effect today.

Much of the modern world has arrayed itself against the nation of Israel. There is constant turmoil in the Middle East, and many of the Arab nations seethe with anger and plot to bring about the destruction of the Jews. But in the long run, God will prove absolutely loyal to His promise of old, and He will bring destruction on those nations that set themselves against Israel. He will also one day bring the Jewish nation to a saving knowledge of the Messiah, Jesus Christ (see Romans 11:26).

REFLECTING ON THE TEXT

5) Why did the people of Gibeon use deception to make peace with Israel? Why did God honor Israel's covenant with them anyway?

_____

_____

_____

6) Why does God command His people to be strong and of good courage? In what way is strength a matter of choice? In what way is courage a matter of choice?

_____

_____

_____

7) Do you believe that God actually caused the earth to stop rotating on its axis for a period of time? Why or why not? What does your response reveal about your faith?

_____

_____

_____

8) Why does God bless those who bless Israel? How does this promise apply today in the ongoing Middle East conflicts?

_____

_____

_____

PERSONAL RESPONSE

9) When you are faced with a crisis, what is your response? How courageous are you? Where do you place your hope for a solution?

_____

_____

_____

10) Do you believe that God, who moved heaven and earth for Israel, stands on your behalf? How can you strengthen your faith in His character?

_____

_____

_____

6

RAISING UP JUDGES

Judges 1:1–2:23

DRAWING NEAR

What is the problem with not getting rid of the things that tempt you? Why is it important to get those things that lead you astray out of your life?

_____

_____

_____

THE CONTEXT

As we have seen, the people of Israel entered the Promised Land with great joy and with tremendous victories. They witnessed the power of their God at work through incredible miracles such as the parting of the Jordan River and the sun standing still, as well as through miraculous victories over their enemies. There could be no doubt the Lord was sovereign and was fighting on their behalf.

In all those great miracles and victories, the Lord had commanded the people to be involved. They had not sat on the sidelines, merely watching the walls of Jericho collapse, but had marched around the city and blown trumpets for seven days. The Lord made the sun stand still and sent huge hailstones to defeat Israel's enemies, but He had also insisted that Israel fight in the battle. God was fighting Israel's battles, but the people still needed to walk in obedience to His commands.

One of those commands had been to drive out all the people of Canaan and tear down their pagan altars. The people got off to a good start under the leadership of Joshua, moving from battle to battle and victory to victory. But as time went along, the various tribes of Israel gradually began to fail. Rather than driving out the Canaanites, they used them as slaves and permitted them to remain in the land.

After Joshua died, the Israelites began a long period of falling into paganism, followed by repentance, followed by a relapse into paganism. During this time the Lord raised up a succession of individuals known as *judges*—men and one woman whom He appointed to lead the nation to victory over its enemies and back toward obedience to God. Yet the cycle of sin and repentance continued.

KEYS TO THE TEXT

Read Judges 1:1–2:23, noting the key words and phrases indicated below.

> *JUDAH TAKES THE LEAD: God had commanded the Israelites to drive out the Canaanites, but they had failed to do so. So God instructs the tribe of Judah to lead in completing the conquest.*

1:1. AFTER THE DEATH OF JOSHUA: Descriptions of the book's setting in Judges 1 and 2 vary between times after Joshua's death (c. 1383 BC) and flashbacks summarizing conditions while he was alive (see, for example, Judges 2:2–6).

2. JUDAH SHALL GO UP: Judah received God's first go-ahead to push for a more thorough conquest of its territory. The reason probably rested in God's choice that Judah be the leader among the tribes and set the example for them in the other territories.

6. CUT OFF HIS THUMBS AND BIG TOES: Removing the king's thumbs hampered effective use of a weapon, while taking off his big toes rendered footing unreliable in battle. Thus, the king was rendered unable to fight or rule effectively in the future. The Lord Himself is nowhere said to endorse this tactic,

but it was an act of retributive justice for what Adoni-Bezek had done to others. It appears from his confession that he was acknowledging that he deserved it.

THE CONQUEST STALLS: *Although Judah makes progress in driving out the remaining Canaanites, the rest of the tribes falter— and the conquest is incomplete.*

12. THEN CALEB SAID: This repeats the account of Caleb and his family as told in Joshua 15:13–19.

16. THE CITY OF PALMS: This refers to the area around Jericho, which had been destroyed during the Israelite invasion. It was an oasis of springs and palms.

19. THEY COULD NOT DRIVE OUT: God had permitted Israel's enemies to hold out in Canaan as a test of whether His people would obey Him. Unfortunately, the tribes would repeatedly fail to rise up and trust in God's power to give them the victory. This tendency to settle for less than what God was able to give had begun in Joshua's day and even earlier.

20. SONS OF ANAK: Anak was an early inhabitant of central Canaan from whom came a group of unusually tall people called the Anakim (see Deuteronomy 2:10). These people had frightened the ten spies, but Caleb had finally driven them out of the land, with the exception of some who resettled with the Philistines.

34. THE AMORITES FORCED THE CHILDREN OF DAN: Like the other tribes, Dan had been given a territory, but they failed to claim the power of God to conquer it. Later, they capitulated even more by accepting defeat and migrating to another territory in the north.

THE LORD DISCIPLINES HIS PEOPLE: *Because the people of Israel fail to obey the Lord, He determines to leave the Canaanites in their land—where their idols will become a snare to them.*

2:1. THE ANGEL OF THE LORD: Once again, the Lord Himself appeared to the people of Israel—but this time His message was not good news.

BOCHIM: This location is not certain, but it may have been near Bethel.

2. YOU SHALL MAKE NO COVENANT WITH THE INHABITANTS OF THIS LAND: The Lord had told the people, "I will set your bounds from the Red

Sea to the sea, Philistia, and from the desert to the River. For I will deliver the inhabitants of the land into your hand, and you shall drive them out before you. You shall make no covenant with them, nor with their gods" (Exodus 23:31–32). The Israelites did not obey the Lord's command in this regard—as we have seen, they had scarcely arrived in the Promised Land when they made a covenant with the people of Gibeon. God had forbidden them to dwell in the land, for he knew their gods would become a snare to His people (see verse 33). And so it was.

YOU SHALL TEAR DOWN THEIR ALTARS: The Lord had made a similar command prior to the battle against Jericho, when He told the people, "By all means abstain from the accursed things, lest you become accursed when you take of the accursed things, and make the camp of Israel a curse, and trouble it" (Joshua 6:18). It was not enough for the Israelites merely to defeat the Lord's enemies in Canaan. They were also to completely destroy anything that pertained to the Canaanites' pagan practices.

YOU HAVE NOT OBEYED MY VOICE: As we have seen, most of the tribes had taken possession of areas of Canaan, but they had failed to drive out the former inhabitants. Many of the Canaanite nations were put under tribute to the tribes of Israel, effectively serving them as slaves. The Israelites may have thought enslaving the people of Canaan was "close enough" to the Lord's command. In fact, it may even have seemed both merciful and prudent to gain labor from them rather than killing them or driving them out. But the Lord had specifically and repeatedly told the people to not make any form of treaty with the Canaanites—not even one involving slavery—and they had disobeyed Him.

3. I WILL NOT DRIVE THEM OUT BEFORE YOU: The people of Israel may have lost sight of the fact that their great victories in battle were the Lord's doing, not their own. It was the Lord who had destroyed Jericho, defeated Ai, made the sun stand still, and caused the Jordan River to part. Yet, as we discussed, He had always commanded the people to participate in some small way. Now they had failed to do even this small part in driving out the Canaanites, so He would withdraw His arm from their future battles as well.

THEIR GODS SHALL BE A SNARE TO YOU: God did not take pleasure in destroying the nations of Canaan, and He did not command His people to do so out of some vindictive or spiteful spirit. The people of Canaan had given themselves fully to paganism and were devoted to all manner of false gods and wicked worship practices, and it was this the Lord wanted to destroy. God is jealous of His people's purity, and He knew the Canaanites' religion would corrupt the Israelites if it were allowed to remain. Thus, He commanded the pagans to be driven out and their idolatrous altars be completely destroyed. The Israelites failed to obey, which opened the door to all manner of corruption.

4. THE PEOPLE LIFTED UP THEIR VOICES AND WEPT: When the people recognized the Lord's hand of discipline was on them, due to their many years of disobedience and indifference, they wept.

5. BOCHIM: Meaning "weepers."

THE NEXT GENERATION: *In addition to failing to drive out the Canaanites, the Israelites have also failed to teach their children about the Lord's character and all He has done for them.*

10. DID NOT KNOW THE LORD: After the Israelites crossed the Jordan River, the Lord commanded them to build a stone monument "that this may be a sign among you when your children ask in time to come, saying, 'What do these stones mean to you?'" (Joshua 4:6). Here we see the reason for that monument, as the subsequent generations in Israel had apparently failed to teach their children about all the Lord had done. It didn't take long before a generation arose who had no knowledge of the Lord's character or the mighty miracles He had performed on behalf of His people. The same trend is happening in our world today.

11. DID EVIL IN THE SIGHT OF THE LORD: This is the natural result of failing to train one's children in the ways of the Lord. If we don't actively teach righteousness to the next generation, they will naturally fall into evil— especially in the pagan ways of the world around them. This generation of Israelites began to worship Baal, a pagan god served by the Canaanites who had not been driven out of the land.

13. BAAL AND THE ASHTORETHS: Baal was one of the chief false deities worshiped in Canaan. He was pictured as standing astride a bull and was thought to provide spring rains and abundant crops. The Ashtoreths were various false goddesses, including Ashtoreth (consort of Baal) and Asherah (wife of Baal's father), who were believed to bring fertility and military strength. The pagan worship rites of all of these counterfeit gods included temple prostitution and even child sacrifice.

14. DELIVERED THEM INTO THE HANDS OF PLUNDERERS: When Israel abandoned the Lord, He delivered Israel to its enemies. This was done not to destroy Israel but to bring the people back to the Lord and to purify them of pagan immorality.

THE LORD RAISES UP JUDGES: Even in the midst of God's discipline, His grace and mercy abound. He raises up judges in Israel to lead His people back to obedience.

16. THE LORD RAISED UP JUDGES: The Lord did send calamity on Israel when the Israelites abandoned Him, but here we see His discipline was meant for the good of His people. He showed His mercy, even in the midst of His discipline, by providing judges who would lead His people back to obedience. These judges were gifted leaders whom God raised up at various times and in a variety of locations. Many of them led Israel's fighting forces to military victory, and some also provided legal judgment among the Israelites. There were six "minor" judges (meaning the Bible gives little detail about them) and six "major" judges (Othniel, Ehud, Deborah, Gideon, Jephthah, and Samson).

17. THEY WOULD NOT LISTEN TO THEIR JUDGES: The people of Israel had a long history of not listening to their God-appointed leaders. They had repeatedly refused to listen to Moses and more than once had risen up in rebellion against his leadership. When God's people reject the leadership He has appointed, they are effectively rejecting the lordship of God Himself.

THEY PLAYED THE HARLOT WITH OTHER GODS: The Lord views idolatry of any kind as a form of spiritual adultery. As His people we belong to Him alone, and we become like an unfaithful wife when we permit anything to come between us and Him.

18. THE LORD WAS MOVED TO PITY BY THEIR GROANING: The Lord sent a series of calamities and hardships to Israel during the period of the judges (roughly 450 years), but His motivation was always to bring His people back to Himself. God does not take pleasure in disciplining His children, and He is always moved to pity when He hears our heartfelt groans.

19. WHEN THE JUDGE WAS DEAD: This represented a continual cycle in Israel during these years. The people would abandon the Lord and run after pagan gods; the Lord would deliver Israel into the hands of her enemies; the people would cry out in despair under the Lord's discipline; the Lord would have mercy and raise up a judge to deliver Israel; the people would obey the Lord for a time; the judge would die . . . and the cycle would begin again. The great wonder of this sequence is that the Lord continued to show grace and patience with such obstinate sinners. Sadly, we are no different from the Israelites, and we must guard against imitating their cycle of sin and repentance.

UNLEASHING THE TEXT

1) Why did God command Israel to not make any covenants with the people of Canaan? What resulted from their failure to obey?

_____

_____

_____

2) Why had the people not driven out the Canaanites as God commanded? What motivated their disobedience?

_____

_____

_____

3) If you had been present when the Angel of the Lord pronounced God's discipline, how would you have reacted? How would it have influenced your life in the future?

_____

_____

_____

4) Why were the people commanded to tear down the Canaanites' altars? What resulted from their failure to do so?

_____

_____

_____

EXPLORING THE MEANING

The world's values can become a snare to God's people. The Lord had commanded the Israelites to completely drive out the people of Canaan because the Canaanites had devoted themselves to pagan practices. Furthermore, He had insisted that Israel destroy the worship sites where the Canaanites had conducted their pagan rites because He knew His people could be seduced into idolatry by long-term contact with those who worshiped idols.

The same principle holds true today. The modern world has increasingly embraced all forms of paganism, and its value system is opposed to the Word of God. As Christians, we can easily be lured away from purity and obedience by the world's emphasis on the pursuit of pleasure, self-worship, sexual immorality, and materialism. The process of embracing those values can be subtle and gradual—a process of small steps that seem innocuous at the time.

The way to stand guard against this danger is to be constantly renewing our minds with the truth. It is vital to spend time daily reading God's Word and talking with Him in prayer. Joining with other Christians on a regular basis for worship and teaching (through involvement with a local church) is also essential. The Holy Spirit is our guard against the pagan influences of the world, but we are called to do our part in obeying the Bible's teachings.

Our present generation is growing up without spiritual guidance. God commanded His people to be faithful in teaching their children about His character and His involvement with Israel. "You shall teach them diligently to your children," He had said, "and shall talk of them when you sit in your house, when you walk by the way, when you lie down, and when you rise up" (Deuteronomy 6:7). But the Israelites gradually forgot to follow this principle, and eventually a generation grew up who didn't know the Lord at all.

The result of this failure was that an entire generation in Israel wandered away from obedience to God and embraced the pagan practices of the world around them. In a way, that was only to be expected, because that generation had not been adequately taught about who God was or what He expected of His people. The parents of that generation had not properly instructed them about God, and thus they were seduced by the pagan religions of Canaan.

Western civilization today is seeing a generation coming to adulthood who know nothing about God's character or what He expects of men and women. These young adults have no root in God's Word and no direction on what the Creator expects of His people, so they naturally follow the pagan teachings of the world around them. It is vital that Christians today be bold in teaching the next generation the truth of the Bible.

Do not fall into a cycle of sin and repentance. The people of Israel had disobeyed the Lord's commands, which led them into idolatry and immorality. The Lord responded by sending hardship on the people as a form of discipline, urging them to return to obedience and purity. The oppression of enemies and other calamities forced Israel to repent and return to the Lord, and He graciously sent judges to lead them back to obedience. But after a time, the people lost interest in the things of God and soon began the cycle all over again.

This cycle was not pleasing to God. He wants His people to obey Him willingly and worship Him voluntarily with their whole hearts. God will send discipline into our lives to make us purer and more like Christ, but His deep desire is for us to obey Him out of love and gratitude rather than by the compulsion of hardship. It is a mark of spiritual maturity to obey God's Word simply because we know that it pleases and glorifies the Father.

REFLECTING ON THE TEXT

5) How might the Israelites have justified their failure to drive out the people of Canaan? In what ways do Christians today sometimes justify disobedience and worldliness?

_____

_____

_____

6) Why did the Lord respond to Israel's disobedience by not driving out the Canaanites? What might have resulted if He had driven them out?

_____

_____

_____

7) Why did a generation grow up without knowing God? What evidence do you see of that trend in the world today? What can be done to correct it?

_____

_____

_____

8) What sorts of "snares" endanger Christians today? How can we guard against them?

_____

_____

PERSONAL RESPONSE

9) What motivates you to obey God's Word? Are you in a cycle of sin and repentance, or do you obey willingly?

_____

_____

_____

10) Are you ensnared with the world's values? What areas in your life might the Lord want you to purify in the coming week?

_____

_____

_____

7

DEBORAH AND BARAK

Judges 4:1–5:31

DRAWING NEAR

Why do you think God rewards those who are courageous for Him? What examples of this have you seen in your life?

_____

_____

_____

THE CONTEXT

In a previous study, we saw how Joshua led the Israelites to a great victory over an alliance of kingdoms that had mobilized to fight against them (see Joshua 11). This enemy federation was led by Jabin, king of Hazor. The name _Jabin_ was probably a title rather than a personal name, similar to the title _Pharaoh_ in Egypt, as we now find another Jabin in Hazor, hundreds of years later. This Jabin, like his predecessor, raised an army to fight against God's people.

The event took place during the time of the judges. Jabin had risen to power and had drawn together a coalition of smaller cities with a powerful army. This army was equipped with a huge force of chariots—_iron_ chariots.

Iron was a relatively new invention at this time, and it was vastly superior to the bronze it replaced. Iron was used not only for swords but also for armor, both for soldiers and for their chariots, which lent formidable strength to a cavalry unit. Israel did not have any iron weapons or armor, and certainly no iron-clad chariots. They were outnumbered and outclassed by the mighty army of Jabin.

Jabin's military advantages gave him the ability to oppress the people of Israel, and he took full advantage of it for twenty years. We do not know the details of his oppression, but it probably involved huge tax burdens for the Israelites as well as oppressive laws restricting their freedoms. The Philistines, for example, made it illegal for Israel to work with iron so their weapons would remain inferior.

The northern tribes of Israel were being led at this time by a judge named Deborah, referred to as "a mother in Israel" (Judges 5:7). She was a woman of wisdom and prudence, and the people of Israel came to her for judgment when settling civil disagreements. The fighting men of Israel were led by Barak, about whom little is known. Barak was probably a man of courage and fighting skill, as he had risen to a position of leadership, but in this study we will discover that even a seasoned fighter can succumb to the sin of fear.

Keys to the Text

Read Judges 4:1–5:31, noting the key words and phrases indicated below.

> GOD RAISES UP DEBORAH: *Israel's repeated disobedience leads the Lord to raise up an enemy for discipline. But soon He also raises up a judge to deliver them: Deborah.*

4:1. EHUD: One of the so-called major judges of Israel (see Judges 3).

THE CHILDREN OF ISRAEL AGAIN DID EVIL IN THE SIGHT OF THE LORD: This is a constant refrain in the book of Judges. The Israelites would fall into wickedness; then the Lord would deliver them into suffering, usually at the hands of the Canaanite nations the people had failed to drive out; the people would then raise their voices in suffering to the Lord; the Lord would respond by raising up a judge to deliver them—and then the cycle would repeat.

2. HAZOR: Located just south of Dan. See the map in the Introduction.

THE COMMANDER OF HIS ARMY WAS SISERA: The general of Jabin's army.

4. DEBORAH . . . WAS JUDGING ISRAEL AT THAT TIME: Deborah was the only woman listed in the Old Testament as a judge in Israel. Indeed, female leadership among God's people was exceedingly rare in Israel. In the New Testament, the principle the Lord has laid down for the church is that men are called to lead.

5. THE CHILDREN OF ISRAEL CAME UP TO HER FOR JUDGMENT: Not all of Israel's judges are said to have "held court" to settle disputes and legal matters, although there were others who did so besides Deborah. Her role as arbiter suggests she had great wisdom. Her name means "bee," and she probably had many beelike qualities: industry, diligence, and prudence, for example.

7. AGAINST YOU I WILL DEPLOY SISERA: This is an interesting picture of God's sovereignty over human affairs. It suggests the Lord was going to act as the commander of the enemy's army, deploying them as He saw fit. This is similar to the way the Lord hardened the heart of Pharaoh before the exodus: Pharaoh had *already* set his heart firmly against God and His people, so the Lord used his hardness of heart to accomplish His own purposes. In the same way, the Lord here was promising that He would turn Sisera's aggression against himself, leading his army into Israel's hands.

BARAK'S UNWILLING LEADERSHIP: The Lord commands Barak to lead His people to victory, but he is afraid to obey. He makes a counteroffer that deprives himself of blessing.

8. IF YOU WILL GO WITH ME, THEN I WILL GO: Barak's response was not pleasing to the Lord, both because it was disobedient and because it demonstrated a lack of faith. The Lord had commanded him to lead the army into battle, and there was no room for negotiations. A military leader does not make bargains with his commanders; he simply obeys his orders.

BUT IF YOU WILL NOT GO WITH ME, I WILL NOT GO: Barak tried to make stipulations on obedience because he did not fully believe the Lord would keep His promise of victory. He needed some form of security to ensure that the Lord would keep His word, and this lack of faith demonstrated that he did not fully trust in the character of God.

9. THE LORD WILL SELL SISERA INTO THE HAND OF A WOMAN: This woman would turn out to be Jael, not Deborah. For Barak's victory to be ascribed to a woman would have been a disgrace, for it was a man's part to lead an army into battle.

10. ZEBULUN AND NAPHTALI: Two tribes of Israel.

11. THE FATHER-IN-LAW OF MOSES: The Kenites were distantly related to the Israelites and had a strong tradition of cooperation and peace with God's people. It was no accident that this man and his family were living near Jabin, for the Lord intended to use them to accomplish His purposes.

13. CHARIOTS OF IRON: This was the dawn of the so-called Iron Age, when iron was a relatively new invention. It was so superior to bronze for weaponry that the Philistines would not allow the Israelites to make it. The armies of Israel, in fact, were generally underequipped in all respects, including their weapons and armor. The prospect of facing a chariot of iron would have been comparable to facing a modern-day tank.

17. SISERA HAD FLED AWAY: The army of Israel had routed Sisera's forces, but their leader had escaped. This would have been an inconclusive victory at best if Sisera had survived, since he might then have raised another army and attacked Israel again. If Barak had not balked at the Lord's command, God would have delivered Sisera into his hand during the battle. But he did not obey completely, so the Lord reserved Sisera for the hand of a woman.

JAEL GAINS THE VICTORY: *Barak has refused to lead the army of Israel, so the Lord gives the victory to an unknown woman.*

THERE WAS PEACE BETWEEN JABIN . . . AND THE HOUSE OF HEBER: The Kenites were noted metalworkers, and it is possible that Heber had made peace with Jabin in order to work on his iron chariots.

18. JAEL WENT OUT TO MEET SISERA: It is probable that Jael was concerned about the outcome of the battle that day, since she had divided loyalties. Her family was at peace with Jabin, yet her clan was at peace with Israel. In this fatal encounter, Jael showed where her true allegiance lay.

INTO THE TENT: It was a severe breach of etiquette for a man other than her husband to enter a woman's tent. Sisera was probably desperate at this moment, willing to hide himself under the protective skirts of a woman in order to save himself. This attitude was similar to Barak's in that Barak was afraid to go into battle without Deborah by his side.

19. SHE OPENED A JUG OF MILK: Sisera requested water, but Jael gave him milk. Milk is not a good thirst quencher on a hot day, especially after a

man has undergone the physical exertions of battle and flight. It is possible that Jael wanted to make Sisera sleepy so that she could carry out her own plan.

21. TOOK A TENT PEG AND . . . A HAMMER: The hammer and tent pegs were used to keep the tents secure. It was a woman's role to set up and take down the tents, so Jael would have been familiar with their use.

DROVE THE PEG INTO HIS TEMPLE: Ordinarily, the laws of hospitality would have required a guest be protected and cared for while in a person's tent. But Jael's loyalties lay with the people of Israel, and she understood she would be helping God's enemies if she harbored Sisera. She was faced with a difficult decision, but she did not hesitate to obey the Lord's command to destroy Sisera and his forces. Once again, she provided a stark contrast to Barak.

THE SONG OF DEBORAH: *Deborah and Barak sing of Israel's victory and of the Lord's great faithfulness to His people.*

5:1. DEBORAH AND BARAK . . . SANG ON THAT DAY: There has been some conjecture over the authorship of this memorable poem, but it seems most likely that it was written by Deborah. The verb *sang* is in the feminine singular, implying that Barak was joining Deborah in a song that she had written.

2. WHEN LEADERS LEAD IN ISRAEL: This concept is important in understanding the period of the judges. There were numerous times when God's chosen leaders were hesitant to take the lead, as we will see again in Gideon's life. Barak refused to take the full responsibility to which the Lord had called him, and as a result, he lost much of the reward that might have been his.

WHEN THE PEOPLE WILLINGLY OFFER THEMSELVES: Notice there are two parts to receiving the Lord's full blessing here: the leaders must lead, and the people must willingly follow. The people of Israel frequently rejected the authority of those whom the Lord placed over them, such as Moses, and at such times He sent discipline on them. God's people would be richly blessed if the leaders would lead (according to God's instructions) and the people would follow.

7. UNTIL I, DEBORAH, AROSE: Compare Judges 4:6–9. The Lord had called Barak to lead the people out of bondage to their enemies, but his refusal meant the credit for the victory would go to a woman. Jael received most of the recognition by defeating Sisera, but here we see that Deborah ultimately was credited with the spiritual leadership in Israel.

9. THE RULERS OF ISRAEL WHO OFFERED THEMSELVES WILLINGLY: Deborah again underscored the importance of leaders who are willing to sacrifice themselves in service to God's people. Note the repetition of the idea of willingness, both in leading and in following. The Lord calls His people to obey with willing hearts rather than grudging spirits.

11. THEY SHALL RECOUNT THE RIGHTEOUS ACTS OF THE LORD: The victory over Israel's enemies ultimately belonged to the Lord rather than to the deeds of men. God demonstrated His faithfulness by bringing about a great victory over Sisera's army, despite the fact that some of His people did not willingly do what they were told.

17. GILEAD STAYED BEYOND THE JORDAN: Some of the tribes of Israel had failed to come to the aid of their brethren in this battle. Their absence was noticed, despite the fact that the Lord brought a great victory without them.

18. WHO JEOPARDIZED THEIR LIVES TO THE POINT OF DEATH: Conversely, those who fought at their own peril were remembered and honored for their faithfulness to God's people. Those who faithfully participate in the Lord's work will be blessed, while those who shirk their responsibilities will deprive themselves of reward.

20. THEY FOUGHT FROM THE HEAVENS: Deborah recognized that the victory came from the Lord, not from Israel's military might.

28. THE MOTHER OF SISERA: It is interesting that the principal characters mentioned in Deborah's song are women—on both sides of the conflict. Note that the song rarely mentions any deeds on the part of Barak.

UNLEASHING THE TEXT

1) In what ways did Sisera's army have the advantage over the army of Israel? How would you have felt if you were in Israel's army? In Sisera's army?

_____

_____

_____

_____

2) How might the outcome of the battle have been different if Barak had fully obeyed God's command?

_____

_____

_____

3) In your opinion, was Jael justified in what she did to Sisera? Why or why not?

_____

_____

_____

4) Why did God deliver Sisera into the hands of Jael? What was wrong with Barak's request to have Deborah join him in leadership?

_____

_____

_____

EXPLORING THE MEANING

Be strong and courageous. We have considered this principle in a previous study, but it is worth reiterating here. The Lord commanded Barak to lead His people into battle, and He even promised that the Israelites would see a great victory. The Lord had made such promises many times before and had never failed to keep them. Yet Barak was hesitant to obey.

We are not told what motivated his hesitancy. Perhaps he felt unqualified to lead the army or thought that Deborah had a better "connection" with the mind of God than he did. Or maybe he was just afraid. Whatever his motivation, fear was the foundation. He was afraid he would fail—or, more accurately, he was afraid that God would fail and that His promises would not come to pass.

While at times fear can motivate a person to take action in a dangerous situation, in the long run it cripples rather than energizes. Fear is based on a lack of trust in God's character and a core belief that He will not keep His promises. Courage is just the opposite—it motivates a Christian to move forward in faith, despite the appearance of circumstances. Courage is based on faith in God's character and a firm belief that He is always faithful. Courage brings freedom and victory, while fear brings bondage and failure.

God calls men to take the lead in the church and home. The Lord called Barak to lead His army into battle, and his hesitancy caused him to lose credit for the great victory that followed. The credit went instead to a woman, which was considered a great disgrace in the social milieu of the ancient Middle East.

Our culture today would not consider it a disgrace for a woman to receive the accolades for such a victory, and we are accustomed to women in all spheres of leadership. It is easy for God's people to assume that the world's ideas of "egalitarianism" apply to the church as well—in fact, the world condemns those who suggest there are some roles to which women are not called. Yet that is the case in God's definition for the church and home: men are called to take the lead, and women are called to submit to their leadership.

The flip side to this is just as important to understand: if men want women to follow, they must be willing to take the lead. If Barak thought it was a disgrace to lose the credit to a woman, then he should have been willing to take the lead in the first place. When men refuse to stand up and lead in the church or home, they must expect that women will fill the void.

Christians are to obey God's commands, not to negotiate for a "better deal." Barak was the leader of Israel's military, and as such he was probably accustomed to having his commands obeyed without argument. After all, a good soldier never talks back to a commanding officer; he carries out commands without comment. It was all the more startling, therefore, when Barak countermanded the direct orders of his Commanding Officer—God Himself.

Picture a general commanding a soldier to move into battle only to have the soldier respond, "I will go into battle as long as you come with me; if you won't come with me, then I won't go." That soldier's career would be short. Yet how much more audacious is it when a believer tries to find ways around simple obedience to God's Word! We do this when we obey only partway, or tell ourselves that we will begin to obey tomorrow, or when we ignore the Holy Spirit's promptings.

The Lord wants His people to obey His Word, and to obey eagerly—not by compulsion. We cannot experience the Lord's full blessing in our lives unless we willingly obey His commands. As Deborah sang, "When leaders lead in Israel, when the people willingly offer themselves, bless the LORD!" (Judges 5:2).

REFLECTING ON THE TEXT

5) What evidence of God's sovereign leadership do you see in the battle against Sisera? How did the Lord arrange events for Israel's victory?

_____

_____

_____

6) Why do you think Barak hesitated to lead the army into battle? Why did he demand that Deborah go with him?

_____

_____

_____

7) What examples of courage do you find in these passages? What examples of fear do you find? What resulted from each?

_____

_____

_____

8) Are you a willing leader? A willing follower? Are there some areas in which God has to coerce you into obedience?

_____

_____

PERSONAL RESPONSE

9) Are you facing life's challenges with courage or with fear? How can you increase your courage in the coming days and weeks?

_____

_____

_____

10) Are you presently trying to negotiate with God? In what areas of your life is He calling you to increased obedience?

_____

_____

_____

8

GIDEON AND THE MIDIANITES
Judges 6:1–40

DRAWING NEAR

What are some ways that you've "tested" God in the past to make sure that what you were hearing was from Him? What do you think really motivated your request?

_____

_____

_____

THE CONTEXT

So far, we have seen instances when foreign armies came against Israel in open battle. But open warfare was not the only threat Israel faced. There were also times when the nation's enemies used tactics similar to those of terrorist groups today—sweeping into the land and quickly out again, destroying crops and cattle and people along the way. That was the situation at the time of Gideon, another of Israel's judges.

As we discovered from previous studies, this situation arose because the people of Israel had wandered away from the Lord and embraced the pagan practices of the world around them. Once again, the people had repented under the oppression of their enemies, and again the Lord raised up a judge to lead them out of bondage. This time, however, we will discover that the judge himself allowed paganism to enter his own home. (We will see this trend even more dramatically in our study on Samson.)

Gideon was evidently from a fairly wealthy family, and he had lived his life tending crops and herds. Israel's enemies at that time were raiding the land and causing such devastation that even a well-off man like Gideon barely had enough food. We meet Gideon as he is skulking about, trying to thresh wheat in secret, and hoping that his enemies will not swoop in and kill him in the process.

The Lord came to Gideon in human form and greeted him as a "man of valor." At first glance this seems incongruous, as Gideon was trying to stay out of sight and avoid any open confrontation. But the Lord had great plans for him because He saw beyond Gideon's timidity and fears. Even so, it would take some time for Gideon to live up to that badge of honor, for he continued to demonstrate his fear by putting the Lord's promises to the test.

KEYS TO THE TEXT

Read Judges 6:1–40, noting the key words and phrases indicated below.

> *LIKE A PLAGUE OF LOCUSTS: The nation of Israel continues the cycle of sin and repentance, and this time the Lord sends marauding Midianites to discipline His people.*

6:1. THE LORD DELIVERED THEM INTO THE HAND OF MIDIAN: The Midianites were a nation of wandering herdsmen who lived east of the Red Sea. They were distant relations of Israel, descended from Abraham and his second wife, Keturah, whom he married after the death of Sarah (see Genesis 25:1–2). Israel had a long and unpleasant history with Midian—it was a group of Midianite merchants who bought Joseph from his brothers and carried him into slavery in Egypt (see Genesis 37:28), and it was the Midianites who hired Balaam to curse Israel (see Numbers 22:7).

2. THE DENS, THE CAVES, AND THE STRONGHOLDS: The Midianites' oppression over Israel was more than mere dictatorship. The Midianites were

raiding, plundering, and murdering the people, and the Israelites were forced to flee for their lives.

5. AS NUMEROUS AS LOCUSTS: A swarm of locusts can sweep across a field and leave it completely stripped of grain with the suddenness and fury of a passing storm. The use of this phrase vividly depicts the absolute devastation the Midianites and their allies were wreaking on Israel's crops.

THEIR CAMELS: This is the first reference in Scripture of camels used in warfare. The camel was first tamed and used in domestic and military functions during the Iron Age, and it is quite possible that Israel had never encountered it in battle before this. The camel could travel great distances in short amounts of time, making it an early example of a long-range military weapon.

RAISING GIDEON: The people cry out to the Lord, and He raises up a man named Gideon to lead them against the Midianites.

6. THE CHILDREN OF ISRAEL CRIED OUT TO THE LORD: The cycle of sin and repentance was being replayed here yet again, but on this occasion the Lord's response was different than in the past.

10. YOU HAVE NOT OBEYED MY VOICE: On this occasion, the Lord sent a prophet to rebuke the people for their constant cycle of sin and disobedience. He reminded them of all He had done in the past to bring them out of slavery in Egypt and give them one miraculous victory after another over in Canaan— and yet they had responded to His great faithfulness by being unfaithful. They had begun to embrace the idolatrous practices of the world around them and were testing His patience in their sin-and-repentance cycle. The Lord warned them that He would not endure their hard-heartedness indefinitely.

11. THE ANGEL OF THE LORD: Here we have another theophany—the Lord Himself appearing in human form.

GIDEON THRESHED WHEAT IN THE WINEPRESS: Wheat was ordinarily threshed on a large wooden floor that was open on all sides, which permitted the wind to carry away the chaff. Grapes, on the other hand, were pressed in small pits carved into rock, which suggests Gideon did not have much wheat to thresh in the first place. It also shows how much the people of Israel lived in dread of the Midianite raiders—they were afraid to be seen with the smallest quantity of food.

12. YOU MIGHTY MAN OF VALOR: This greeting may seem ironic at first. Gideon was anything but a man of courage at this point, for he was hiding away under a tree to keep his grain out of view. But the Lord was not looking at what he was; rather, He was interested in what Gideon would become under His transforming hand.

13. THE LORD HAS FORSAKEN US: Gideon had an imperfect understanding of God's character. He accused the Lord of having forsaken His people, in spite of God's reiterated promise that He would never do so (see Deuteronomy 4:31). His question of why the Lord had delivered Israel into the hands of Midian indicated that he also failed to recognize the sinful and disobedient condition of his nation.

14. THE LORD TURNED TO HIM: God turned His face on Gideon and showed him great favor and honor. In that moment, evidently, Gideon's eyes were opened and he realized that he was in the presence of the Lord.

GO IN THIS MIGHT OF YOURS: The Lord had just told Gideon that He was with him and that He would cause him to become a "mighty man of valor" (verse 12), but Gideon had remained in doubt. Here God was encouraging Gideon to step out in faith and trust that He had given him a new level of strength and courage. These gifts would ultimately be from the Lord, but to receive them, Gideon first had to take action.

GIDEON'S DOUBTS: *The Lord commands Gideon to be a man of valor, but Gideon responds with doubts and fears.*

15. HOW CAN I SAVE ISRAEL: On one hand, it is understandable that Gideon reacted this way. He was a humble man who recognized his weaknesses and shortcomings. Yet the Lord's response to him was, "You can do what I am commanding, because I will be with you, and I shall enable you to accomplish it." Gideon's doubts arose because he did not trust the Lord to fight the battle for him; he envisioned himself fighting the battle in his own strength. The principle is the same for Christians today: the Lord gives us the power needed to carry out His commands.

17. SHOW ME A SIGN: On the surface, it might almost seem reasonable for Gideon to make these requests to the Lord. After all, it was unusual for the Lord to appear to a man, and the command He was giving was potentially disastrous for all of Gideon's people if it turned out to not be from God. But in

the long run, it will become apparent that Gideon was merely stalling, hoping to find a way around simple obedience to the Lord.

18. DO NOT DEPART FROM HERE: This scene was repeated in almost every detail many years later when the angel of the Lord appeared to the parents of Samson.

19. UNLEAVENED BREAD FROM AN EPHAH OF FLOUR: Gideon prepared a sacrificial offering for the Lord. It was also a generous offering—especially in a time of famine—since an ephah was approximately twenty pounds of flour.

22. I HAVE SEEN THE ANGEL OF THE LORD FACE TO FACE: Gideon was filled with fear because he realized he had been speaking with the Lord Himself, in person—and he knew the Lord had once told Moses, "You cannot see My face; for no man shall see Me, and live" (Exodus 33:20). Yet even in this response, Gideon demonstrated his lack of understanding of God's character. The Lord had appeared to him specifically to promise that He would not destroy him, but rather would be with him and give him great victory.

GIDEON'S FIRST ASSIGNMENT: Before Gideon can lead God's people into battle against Midian, he must first cleanse his own house of idolatry.

25. TEAR DOWN THE ALTAR OF BAAL . . . AND CUT DOWN THE WOODEN IMAGE: This command gives us insight into the spiritual condition of Israel in Gideon's time. His own father had built an altar to a pagan god and was evidently offering sacrifices to Baal. The wooden image was probably a pole set up in honor of the pagan goddess Asherah, a common element of idolatry in Canaan. The Lord had expressly forbidden His people to engage in such idolatrous practices, and He had further commanded His people to destroy the pagan altars of those already living in Canaan (see Exodus 34:13). Yet they had gone so far into disobedience as to build altars of their own.

26. BUILD AN ALTAR TO THE LORD YOUR GOD: This seems to suggest that Gideon did not have an altar for the Lord, or at least not one that was constructed "in the proper arrangement" (Exodus 20:25). It is significant that the Lord commanded Gideon to get his own house in order before leading Israel in battle against Midian. The Lord calls His people to the same priorities today: we must cleanse our own lives of idolatry and disobedience before we can be effective in bringing the gospel to others.

SNEAKING AROUND AT NIGHT: Gideon obeys the Lord's
commands to tear down his father's pagan shrine—but he does it
under cover of darkness because he is afraid.

27. HE DID IT BY NIGHT: Gideon finally demonstrated the true motive for his previous hesitations: fear. As we have seen, fear leads people away from God, not toward Him. Gideon feared his neighbors more than he trusted God's faithfulness. Nevertheless, in spite of his overwhelming trepidation, Gideon still obeyed.

30. BRING OUT YOUR SON: This suggests that Gideon went into hiding after obeying the Lord's command. The people's response did lend some credence to Gideon's fears, as they were so outraged they demanded his death. The dreadful irony was that it was the people of the city who deserved to be stoned to death for their unfaithfulness and idolatry (see Deuteronomy 13:6–10).

31. JOASH SAID TO ALL WHO STOOD AGAINST HIM: It is rather sad that Joash the idolater had more courage than Gideon, the one called by God. But the Lord was not finished with Gideon. He would eventually make him into a man of courage, as He prophesied in their first meeting.

32. JERUBBAAL: Literally, "Let Baal plead." Joash gave his son this nickname in derision of the Canaanite idolaters, who prayed to a nonexistent god who could not even defend his own altar—never mind care for the people who prayed there.

34. THE SPIRIT OF THE LORD CAME UPON GIDEON: This powerful phrase literally means that the Spirit of the Lord clothed Gideon. It suggests that God Himself took control of the ensuing battle, fighting on behalf of His people.

FLEECING GOD: Even after the victory over his idolatrous
neighbors, Gideon is still afraid. The Lord has told him what to do,
but he seeks further proof that God will be faithful.

36. IF YOU WILL SAVE ISRAEL BY MY HAND: In spite of the powerful presence of the Holy Spirit, Gideon was still fearful. He was still struggling to believe that God would keep His promise and bring about a great victory.

37. I SHALL PUT A FLEECE OF WOOL: To this day, people sometimes speak about "putting out a fleece" to gain guidance from the Lord. It is important to understand, however, that Gideon's actions were motivated by a

lack of faith, not by a desire to seek wise counsel. The Lord did not reprimand Gideon for his uncertainty—in fact, He graciously granted him the reassurance that he sought—yet this approach to God's commands is not a model for us to follow.

39. LET ME TEST: Gideon himself recognized that his fleece tests were not in accordance with God's will—note that he asked the Lord to not become angry with him. God had commanded His people to not put Him to the test (see Deuteronomy 6:16; the word translated *tempt* is the same as *test* here), yet Gideon was doing just that—testing the Lord to see whether He would and could keep His promises. Nevertheless, the Lord demonstrated His great grace and patience by performing what Gideon requested.

UNLEASHING THE TEXT

1) When have you been faced with a situation that overwhelmed you? How did you respond? How would you respond now if you were to face those same circumstances?

_____

_____

_____

_____

2) Why did Gideon ask for signs from God? What did this reveal about his faith? About God's character?

_____

_____

_____

3) Why did the Lord command Gideon to destroy his father's pagan altar? Why was this important to do first before fighting the Midianites?

_____

_____

4) Why did Gideon destroy the altar at night? What was the result of his obedience?

_____

_____

_____

EXPLORING THE MEANING

Ask God for guidance, but don't put Him to the test. The Scriptures abound with men and women who were faced with difficult decisions and turned to the Lord for guidance. Jesus urged His disciples to seek the Father's will in all things, teaching them to pray, "Your will be done on earth as it is in heaven" (Matthew 6:10). Today, Christians receive the indwelling of the Holy Spirit, whose role in part is to guide us into all truth (see John 16:13). There is no need to "test" God in order to receive direction.

It is important to recognize in Gideon's story that he was not really seeking guidance by putting out his fleeces. The Lord had already given him guidance and told him exactly what to do, but Gideon was afraid. He feared the Lord would not keep His promises, so he sought miraculous verification of God's faithfulness. The Lord had repeatedly proven Himself faithful throughout Israel's history—parting the Jordan River for them to cross, bringing down the walls of Jericho, giving His people one victory after another against powerful enemies—and Gideon should have rested in faith that the Lord would keep His word once again.

Christians today also have a record of God's faithfulness through the ages. We learn of it through the Bible as we read the testimonies of those who have walked with Him in the past. If we live in light of God's Word and obey the truth He has revealed to us in Scripture, we can do so with confidence, knowing God will be faithful in the present just as He was in the past.

Do not fear what man may do. Gideon lived in terrifying times. His nation was under such oppression and persecution that they did not have enough food to eat, and they were in constant fear for their lives. From a human perspective, it is easy to understand why Gideon would have been afraid to go into battle against Israel's powerful enemies or even to take a bold stand against the idolatry of his family and neighbors. After all, he was not a trained soldier and evidently had lived his life looking after the family's crops and herds.

Interestingly, David had a similar background and faced a comparable situation—yet his response to the Lord's commands was vastly different from Gideon's. David, the youthful shepherd with no military experience, boldly confronted the giant Goliath, the Philistine army's most seasoned champion. Both David and Gideon faced terrifying foes, but it was the Lord who fought the battles in both cases.

David wrote, "I called on the LORD in distress; the LORD answered me and set me in a broad place. The LORD is on my side; I will not fear. What can man do to me?" (Psalm 118:5–6). Hebrews 13:5–6 tells us, "[God] Himself has said, 'I will never leave you nor forsake you.' So we may boldly say: 'The Lord is my helper; I will not fear. What can man do to me?'"

The spiritual battle begins at home. The Lord raised up Gideon to drive out the marauders from Midian, and God eventually brought about a great victory for Israel's forces under Gideon's leadership. But first Gideon had to address the idolatry in his own home. The Lord commanded him to begin by tearing down his father's pagan altar and replacing it with a proper altar at which to worship the God of Israel.

This small battle on the homefront was important for Gideon in several ways. It gave him a taste of battle and taught him that he could trust the Lord. It increased his boldness in obeying the Lord's commands and taught him that he didn't need to fear the unrighteous wrath of his neighbors. Most important, it put him in right relationship with God as he removed the idols from his own house and set up a proper place of worship.

The same principle applies to God's people today. We are called to be salt and light in the world, a living testimony to the truth of the gospel. But our testimony cannot be effective if we are not living in obedience to God's Word— sinful habits and open disobedience dim our light and make our salt lose its savor. "You are the salt of the earth," Jesus told us, "but if the salt loses its flavor, how shall it be seasoned? It is then good for nothing but to be thrown out and trampled underfoot by men" (Matthew 5:13).

REFLECTING ON THE TEXT

5) Why did the Lord send a prophet to the people before raising up Gideon to defeat the Midianites? What does this suggest about the Lord's patience with persistent sin?

_____

_____

_____

_____

6) Why did God refer to Gideon as a "mighty man of valor"? How would you have described him at that point in his life?

_____

_____

_____

7) What is the difference between asking God for guidance and putting Him to the test?

_____

_____

_____

8) What seemed to be Gideon's greatest concern in this story? How might his life have been different if he had trusted the Lord more?

_____

_____

_____

PERSONAL RESPONSE

9) In what areas are you currently seeking God's wisdom for decisions you are facing? How are you applying biblical principles to those decisions? Are you eagerly following those principles, or do you find yourself putting God's Word to the test?

_____

_____

_____

10) Do you tend to fear what people will say or do if you openly obey the Lord's commands? How can you increase your faith and trust in God this week?

_____

_____

_____

9

SAMSON AND THE PHILISTINES
Judges 15:1–16:31

DRAWING NEAR

What is the issue with being complacent with the ways of the world? How do Christians often fall into this particular trap?

_____

_____

_____

THE CONTEXT

Our passage for this study opens many years after Gideon had judged Israel, at a time when the Philistines had become the overlords of the nation. The Philistines were a seafaring people who had probably moved into Canaan from the Greek islands over time. Today we use the term *philistine* to refer to someone who is uncouth, but that does not describe the people who lived during the time of the judges. On the contrary, they were a wealthy and powerful civilization, and their armies were feared around the world. Even the great Egypt could not defeat them.

The Philistines were not tyrannical in the sense of imposing harsh laws, punishments, or enslavement. Instead, they ruled by economic means, imposing taxes and a few laws on the people while still permitting them to live with some measure of autonomy. The people of Israel were kept on a leash, but it was a golden leash. In fact, the Israelites experienced a measure of comfort and economic wealth during this time. It was an easy yoke to bear.

That was part of the problem: the Israelites were becoming too comfortable under the dominion of their heathen neighbors. They were slipping into a state of spiritual lethargy and were in danger of becoming just one more pagan nation in Canaan. They were embracing the pagan practices of the world around them, and the Lord would not tolerate such apostasy from His people. So God raised up yet another judge to lead His people.

However, this time God's plan was not to defeat the enemy in one open battle. Instead, He used this judge to stir up trouble between Israel and the Philistines, wake up His people from their spiritual stupor, and force them to recognize their grave danger. This was the calling of Samson, a man raised as a Nazirite—one who took a vow of purity, made evident to the world by his abstinence from wine, avoiding dead bodies, and never cutting his hair. Samson was called to a life of purity and power. Unfortunately, he did not live up to that calling.

Keys to the Text

Read Judges 15:1–16:31, noting the key words and phrases indicated below.

> THE PHILISTINES' REVENGE: *We pick up Samson's story when he is judge in Israel. He attacks the Philistines and then goes off to a cave. The Philistines come looking for revenge.*

15:1. WHEAT HARVEST: The events in this passage would have taken place in May or June.

SAMSON: The Lord had appeared to Samson's parents before he was born, prophesying that their son would one day deliver God's people from Philistine oppression. They were given strict instructions that he was to live under the strictures of the Nazirite vow. Samson was forbidden to drink wine, touch any dead body, or cut his hair. By the time our passage begins, however, he had grown to manhood—and already violated two of the three stipulations by getting drunk and touching a lion's carcass.

2. I REALLY THOUGHT: Shortly after Samson's ill-conceived marriage to a Philistine woman, his father-in-law gave his new bride to his best man (see Judges 14). When Samson returned and asked to see his wife, his father-in-law gave a flimsy excuse to escape the trap he faced. He feared the Philistines if he turned on the new husband, yet he also feared Samson, so he offered his second daughter as a way out. This action set up the events that followed.

4. CAUGHT THREE HUNDRED FOXES: Samson, insulted and provoked to resentment, took vengeance on the Philistines. Apparently, he tied the foxes in pairs by their tails, then attached slow-burning torches, and sent them into the fields. This was a loss of great proportion to the Philistine farmers.

6. BURNED HER AND HER FATHER: The general principle of reaping what is sown was at work here (see Galatians 6:7).

8. ATTACKED THEM HIP AND THIGH: This is proverbial for a ruthless slaughter.

9. THE PHILISTINES: The Philistine nation comprised five major city-states: Gath, Ashkelon, Ashdod, Ekron, and Gaza. The modern-day Gaza strip is built on the Philistine city.

LEHI: Meaning "jawbone." The exact location is not known, but it probably received this name after Samson's great slaughter there.

BINDING THE STRONG MAN: *The men of Judah simply want to live in peace with the Philistines—even if it means betraying their own judge to maintain that peace.*

11. THREE THOUSAND MEN OF JUDAH: This was a strong response to the situation, and it indicates Samson's strength was already well known. The response of so many men of Judah also suggests they had grown quite comfortable under the oppression of the Philistines. Their question, "Do you not know that the Philistines rule over us?" indicates they were content to leave things as they were. But that was not the Lord's plan for His people.

AS THEY DID TO ME, SO I HAVE DONE TO THEM: There is ample room for doubt about the accuracy of this statement. The Philistines had cheated Samson at his own wedding feast, and his father-in-law had given his bride to another man after Samson.

DISAPPEARED FOR A PERIOD OF TIME: Samson's actions had been excessive and bloody. After collecting payment for the bet he had lost by murdering thirty people in a Philistine city, he had slaughtered more Philistines and burned their crops in retaliation for losing his wife to another man. The Lord was using Samson's actions to move the Israelites out of their complacency under Philistine rule, yet Samson's life was no model of godliness.

12. THAT WE MAY DELIVER YOU: The men of Judah were guilty of treachery in this action. They should have banded together under the leadership of God's chosen judge and fought against the Philistines instead of cooperating with them to deliver one of their own to the oppressor. This demonstrates that the people of Israel were growing dangerously complacent, content to follow the world around them rather than obey God's commands.

13. TWO NEW ROPES: New ropes would have been stronger and more reliable than ropes that had been used before. The fact that the men used two ropes suggests that Samson's arms were bound tightly to his side, the ropes twining about his torso and possibly even constricting his legs. The men of Judah were not taking chances, yet their confidence was placed in the wrong direction—they trusted two little ropes rather than God.

GOD'S POWER UNLEASHED: *The Spirit of the Lord comes on Samson, and he is transformed into a superhuman fighter. No army can stand before him.*

14. THE SPIRIT OF THE LORD CAME MIGHTILY: The Lord's Spirit manifested His power in a unique way in Samson's life by giving him superhuman physical strength. The anointing of the Holy Spirit was rare prior to the ascension of Christ. The Spirit came on men temporarily, enabling them to accomplish something beyond their human powers, but did not necessarily remain with them indefinitely. This is one of the many great gifts the Lord has provided to His children today through Christ. Christians are *permanently* indwelt by the person of God's Holy Spirit.

LIKE FLAX THAT IS BURNED WITH FIRE: The two new ropes proved laughable when the Spirit came on Samson. The men of Judah may not have recognized that it was the power of God, not the power of a man, that was filling Samson—for binding the Holy Spirit with rope is like trying to stop a locomotive with a piece of thread. The power of man cannot prevent the purposes of God, though man is capable of abusing God's gifts, as we will see in Samson's life.

15. A FRESH JAWBONE OF A DONKEY: This was evidently from a donkey that had died fairly recently. The sun would have quickly dried out the bone, making it brittle and of little use as a weapon. Once again, we see Samson touching a dead body, directly against his Nazirite vow.

KILLED A THOUSAND MEN: The Lord had placed Samson under a special set of regulations, including the provision that he not touch anything dead, and Samson had persistently ignored those rules. Yet the Lord, within His providential purposes, chose to use Samson in spite of his shortcomings to perform miraculous feats against Israel's enemies. Samson single-handedly stirred up the people of Israel to rise against the Philistine oppression. Nonetheless, that conflict would not be completed until the time of David.

16. HEAPS UPON HEAPS: This is a pun, as the Hebrew word for *heap* is similar to the word for *donkey*.

19. GOD SPLIT THE HOLLOW PLACE: Samson's life was not characterized by faithful obedience, yet the Lord continually showed him grace and met his needs.

SAMSON MEETS A PROSTITUTE: *Samson's flesh now leads him further down the path to destruction, yet the Lord still uses him to plague the Philistines.*

16:1. GAZA: One of the five major Philistine cities, site of the modern city of Gaza. Each Philistine city had a standing army of its own, and they were the best-trained and best-equipped fighting forces in Canaan at the time.

SAW A HARLOT: Samson's physical lusts were leading him down a course to ruin.

3. THE DOORS OF THE GATE OF THE CITY AND THE TWO GATEPOSTS: The city of Gaza was probably constructed with a double wall surrounding it, similar to Jericho. There would have been a high-vaulted passageway between the walls, with heavy gates set into the outer wall constructed of thick wood reinforced with iron. The gates would be locked at night with a huge oak beam set into iron brackets (the "bar" referred to here). The gate posts would have been set into the walls themselves, and the entire structure was designed to withstand a besieging army and its battering rams. There was simply no possibility that one man could have ripped those gates out of the walls. Yet

Samson ripped them down, hoisted them onto his shoulders—a mass of architecture more than ten feet tall and weighing several tons—and carried them to the hill facing Hebron, a city that was some thirty-eight miles away uphill!

ENTER DELILAH: *Samson's fleshly indulgences finally bring him into contact with Delilah, who works for the Philistines. It will lead to Samson's downfall.*

4. DELILAH: Delilah was probably a Philistine. She was certainly not a Hebrew, and Samson had no business becoming involved with her. She is renowned in literature and art as a deadly seductress, but the fault of Samson's fate lay more with Samson than with her.

5. FIND OUT WHERE HIS GREAT STRENGTH LIES: The world marveled at the superhuman feats Samson had performed, and evidently only Samson recognized that the power came directly from God. Yet, as we will see, even Samson did not fully comprehend these miracles, as he attributed God's indwelling to some mystical connection with his long hair—the one stipulation of his Nazirite vow that he had not yet disobeyed.

6. PLEASE TELL ME WHERE YOUR GREAT STRENGTH LIES: Thus began the tragic downfall of Samson, as Delilah repeatedly questioned him and he repeatedly deceived her. It seems incredible that a man of his stature would fail to recognize that she was in the service of the Philistine lords, and was trying to seduce his secret for his own destruction. Yet Samson's life had not been characterized by wisdom; he had repeatedly violated the word of God and had used the Lord's great gifts for his own purposes. A lifetime of folly will lead one to ever greater folly, even to the point of self-destruction.

9. THE SECRET OF HIS STRENGTH WAS NOT KNOWN: The interesting thing is that so far as we know, the Lord never instructed Samson to keep his strength a secret. The Lord filled Samson with His Holy Spirit specifically so Samson might bring to deliverance to God's people, and it would have been far more effective if Samson had publicly proclaimed that his great strength came directly from the Spirit of God. But, as we have seen, Samson was more interested in using that gift to gratify his own desires.

16. HIS SOUL WAS VEXED TO DEATH: The sequence of seduction apparently continued for some time, perhaps over many months. Samson had placed himself in the power of the enemy by involving himself in an immoral

relationship with Delilah, which gave her the ability to nag him, goad him, and seduce him until he couldn't stand to hear it any longer. His only hope was to repent of his sinful habits, abandon Delilah, and purify his life—but he failed to do that, and ultimately his spiritual strength wore out. His physical strength followed close behind.

17. THEN MY STRENGTH WILL LEAVE ME: There is no indication that Samson's strength was directly tied to his long hair. Rather, his hair was an outward symbol of his own submission to the Spirit of God. The one element of Samson's statement that is accurate is his comment that he would "be like any other man" if his hair were cut, as it would represent his final act of rebellion against God's commands.

HE DID NOT KNOW THAT THE LORD HAD DEPARTED:
Samson makes his final choice to betray his Nazirite vows, and the Spirit of God leaves him. But not forever.

20. HE DID NOT KNOW THAT THE LORD HAD DEPARTED: This is one of the saddest statements in Scripture. It indicates Samson had taken the Lord's presence for granted and had no intimate relationship with the God of Israel. He was not even aware when God's Spirit had left.

22. THE HAIR OF HIS HEAD BEGAN TO GROW AGAIN: This should not be construed to mean that as Samson's hair grew, so did his miraculous physical strength. During his time in prison, Samson evidently had time to reflect on his life and his divine calling.

25. BETWEEN THE PILLARS: Archeologists have unearthed Philistine temples that were similar to the one in Gaza. They were constructed with two major pillars near the center, which bore most of the weight. The temple in Gaza evidently included an open courtyard surrounded by a multi-storied temple. The lords and ladies, comfortably seated in surrounding balconies, watched Samson perform like a trained circus animal in the courtyard.

28. SAMSON CALLED TO THE LORD: In this brief prayer, Samson referred to the Lord by three different names: *Adonai, Yahweh,* and *Elohim.* This suggests he had come to a fuller appreciation of God's character during his time of imprisonment and had fully repented of his sins. Ironically, he needed to have his physical eyes gouged out to open his spiritual eyes.

Unleashing the Text

1) How would you characterize Samson's life? What were his great strengths? What were his great weaknesses?

_____

_____

_____

2) Why did the Lord empower Samson to slaughter three thousand Philistines? Why did He enable him to tear the gates from Gaza? What was He working to accomplish?

_____

_____

_____

3) What was the "secret" of Samson's great strength? What does this teach you about God's involvement in the lives of His people?

_____

_____

_____

4) Why did Samson tell Delilah how to enslave him? What led him to that point? Why did he not foresee what would happen?

_____

_____

_____

EXPLORING THE MEANING

The Lord does not abandon us when we sin, but sin can ruin our lives. It is somewhat surprising to read about the life of Samson, so plagued with fleshly indulgence, and realize the Spirit of God continued to use him in mighty ways. He appears to have spent much of his life consorting with the enemies of his people. He indulged in wine despite his Nazirite vow to refrain from it. He married a Canaanite woman, which was forbidden of God's people. He even hired prostitutes and carried on an immoral relationship with Delilah. Yet the Lord used him to begin the overthrow of the Philistines.

The sad fact is that Samson's effectiveness was greatly limited by his own sin and selfishness. Instead of being both a political leader and a spiritual example in Israel, he was a moral failure who accomplished far less than his potential. Although Samson would make a dent in Philistine control over Israel, they would not be entirely defeated until a man named David appeared who had a whole heart for God. The Lord used Samson to accomplish a small part of His plan, but his sinful habits prevented him from accomplishing much more.

The Lord does not abandon His children when we sin, but our sinful habits can severely interfere with our effectiveness in His service. Our sin grieves the Holy Spirit and quenches His power in our lives. When we walk in ungodliness, we risk ending in tragedy, just as Samson did.

The Lord restores those who repent. Samson lived his life indulging every desire of his flesh, with no apparent remorse. He squandered his great gift of strength in many ways, using it for personal revenge and to get himself out of scrapes. He ignored his great calling to lead Israel out of bondage, and as far as we know he never made any attempt to lead the men of Judah into battle. He violated his Nazirite vows and flagrantly disobeyed many of the Lord's injunctions against immoral behavior.

Yet at the end of his life, he repented and turned back to the Lord—and the Lord used him for the mightiest and most dramatic accomplishment of all. Samson had tragically lost many opportunities to accomplish great deeds for the Lord, but that did not prevent the Lord from restoring him to service.

This is the good news that follows the bad news in our previous principle. Sin can damage our lives and limit our effectiveness in God's service. But that does not mean God has washed His hands of us—the Lord is always at work to bring us back into full fellowship with Him, making us fit vessels for His service. As long as we have the breath of life, we have the opportunity to make ourselves right with God. He will always restore those who genuinely repent of sin, and He will use us for His glory. "If we confess our sins, He is faithful and just to forgive us our sins and to cleanse us from all unrighteousness" (1 John 1:9).

Christians have the Spirit of God living within them. Samson believed his great strength came from some magical effect of never cutting his hair. He did not seem to understand that his power came from the Spirit of God, who had chosen to indwell him. When he unintentionally permitted Delilah to cut his hair, he was making a public statement repudiating his Nazirite vows and declaring that the God of Israel was not his Lord. His life was ruled by his own passions.

The same Holy Spirit who empowered Samson also indwells every Christian. The Holy Spirit, of course, is not an impersonal force. Rather, He is a divine Person, who as the third member of the Trinity is coequal and consubstantial with the Father and the Son. The Bible teaches that the Spirit has all of the attributes of personality and deity, including intellect, emotions, volition, eternality, omnipresence, omniscience, omnipotence, and truthfulness. In the church age, which began on the day of Pentecost recorded in Acts 2, the Spirit indwells believers, having regenerated them from sin and sealed them for future glory.

The Spirit also sanctifies, instructs, illuminates, and empowers believers for spiritual service. He enables them to be obedient to the truth. When we walk in accord with the Word of God, which the Holy Spirit inspired, we walk according to the Spirit and thereby exhibit the fruit of the Spirit. On the flip side, when we gratify the desires of our sinful nature (as Samson did), we quench the Spirit and exhibit the fruit of the flesh (see Galatians 5:16–25).

REFLECTING ON THE TEXT

5) Why did God continue to use Samson through so many years of disobedience? Why did the Spirit leave Samson when he cut his hair?

_____

_____

_____

6) Why is Samson listed among the great heroes of the faith in Hebrews 11? What does this suggest about the grace of God?

_____

_____

_____

7) How do you think Samson's life might have been different if he had walked in godliness?

_____

_____

_____

8) What principles of the conflict between flesh and spirit are illustrated in Samson's life? What principles of God's love are illustrated?

_____

_____

_____

PERSONAL RESPONSE

9) Is there an area of sin in your life that is hindering your walk with the Lord? What will you do about it this week?

_____

_____

_____

10) How is the Spirit of God at work in your life at present? How will you
submit yourself to His Word this week?

_____

_____

_____

10

RUTH AND BOAZ
Ruth 1:1–2:23

DRAWING NEAR

Ruth is a model of faithfulness in the Bible. Who is someone who has proven to be faithful to you? What impact has that person's faithfulness had on your life?

_____

_____

_____

THE CONTEXT

The people of Israel had been living in the Promised Land for several generations, during the time known as the period of the judges, when the land of Judah experienced a famine. No further details are known about this crisis, yet we do know it was severe enough for a man named Elimelech to move his family to the land of Moab, east of the Dead Sea.

The Moabites were descendants of Lot from an incestuous union with his oldest daughter (see Genesis 19). Their relations with Israel had not been good, and the Lord had forbidden the Moabites from entering the congregation. Yet Elimelech moved his wife and two sons there—and married his sons to Moabite women.

Many years later, after Elimelech's death, his widow, Naomi, returned to Judah and arrived during the barley harvest. The harvest was a time of hard physical labor, involving cutting the grain by hand, binding it into sheaves, and threshing out the edible grain from the chaff. During this process, the poor were permitted to walk through harvested fields and pick up any bits of grain left behind by the harvesters.

The law of Moses required farmers to leave behind certain portions of grain for the sake of the poor who would come to glean. However, it did not require farmers to feed the gleaners or to pay them any special attention—to do that would be to go above and beyond the call of duty. It is in this setting that we meet Ruth and Boaz. The two were destined to be together—literally a match made in heaven. Through their descendants, God would bring about the human birth of His Son, Jesus Christ.

KEYS TO THE TEXT

Read Ruth 1:1–2:23, noting the key words and phrases indicated below.

TWO WEDDINGS AND THREE FUNERALS: A family moves to Moab to escape famine and the sons marry Moabite women. The men die, leaving three widows behind.

1:1. MOAB: The land of Moab was east of the Dead Sea (see the map in the Introduction). The passage does not tell us whether Elimelech was justified in moving to Moab, as he was effectively leaving the Promised Land to live with the Canaanites.

FAMINE IN THE LAND: Similar disasters occurred in the days of Abraham (see Genesis 12), Isaac (see Genesis 26), and Jacob (see Genesis 46). The text does not specify whether or not this famine was God's judgment.

BETHLEHEM: Literally "house of bread." This city was in the territory given to the tribe of Judah, about six miles south of Jerusalem, and would eventually receive the title "city of David." Later, it would become the site where Mary delivered Christ and Herod slaughtered the infants.

2. ELIMELECH: His name means "my God is king," signifying a devout commitment to the God of Israel. Most likely he was a prominent man in the

community whose brothers might have included the unnamed close relative and Boaz (see Ruth 4:3).

NAOMI: Her name means "pleasant."

MAHLON AND CHILION: Their names mean "sick" and "pining," respectively.

EPHRATHITES: A title used for people who lived in the area more anciently known as Ephrath or Ephrathah, but later more prominently called Bethlehem.

4. THEY TOOK WIVES OF THE WOMEN OF MOAB: The Lord had expressly forbidden the Israelites from marrying Canaanites (see Deuteronomy 7:1–3), and the Moabites in particular were excluded from the congregation of Israel (see 23:3–6). These marriages were questionable at best, but nevertheless the Lord would bring great good out of one of them.

ORPAH: Her name means "stubborn."

RUTH: Her name means "friendship."

ABOUT TEN YEARS: This seems to include the entire time of Naomi's residency in Moab.

5. THE WOMAN SURVIVED HER TWO SONS AND HER HUSBAND: This tragedy would have been grievous enough for anyone to endure, but Naomi's sorrow was compounded by the fact she had no sons to carry on the family name.

6. THE LORD HAD VISITED HIS PEOPLE: The sovereignty of God is seen throughout this book, as the Lord worked to bring about a good end to these tragic events.

7. SHE WENT OUT: Naomi had friends, family, and prosperity awaiting her in Bethlehem.

PARTING COMPANY: Naomi urges her daughters-in-law to return to their own families and find husbands for themselves.

8. RETURN EACH TO HER MOTHER'S HOUSE: Orpah and Ruth were Moabites and therefore had no place in the congregation of Israel. It was only natural that they should return to their families and remain in the land of Moab. Naomi at this point looked forward only to returning to Judah as a lonely widow, bereft of any offspring. Her future was bleak.

11. TURN BACK, MY DAUGHTERS: Naomi was being selfless in urging her daughters-in-law to go home to Moab. It would have been a comfort to have

their company on the return trip to Judah, but she was more concerned for their future and welfare. She wanted them to find husbands and have families to carry on their family heritage.

12. I AM TOO OLD: Naomi was probably over fifty.

13. THE HAND OF THE LORD HAS GONE OUT AGAINST ME: This is a figure of speech that describes the Lord's work. We can understand the terrible grief Naomi must have been suffering at this time, yet her perspective was inaccurate. The Lord had *not* set His hand against her, as later events would make clear. Though unpleasant in the short-term, God uses suffering and trials to make His people more like Himself (see 1 Peter 1:6–7).

15. BACK TO HER PEOPLE AND HER GODS: At the second plea to return, Orpah turned back. Her decision to return to Moab probably seemed prudent at the time, as it was more likely she would find a husband and family there. But the bigger issue is that her return to Moab was also a return to Moab's gods, and was thus a rejection of the God of Israel. The chief deity of Moab was Chemosh, whose worship included child sacrifice.

RUTH REMAINS: Orpah returns to her family in Moab, but Ruth refuses to leave the side of her mother-in-law. In her faithfulness, she is willing to abandon everything.

16. WHEREVER YOU GO, I WILL GO: Ruth's words expressed a complete commitment to remain with Naomi regardless of her circumstances.

YOUR GOD, MY GOD: Ruth recognized her decision included a resolve to forsake the gods of Moab and instead embrace the God of Israel. This conversion had consequences for the entire human race, as her family line would ultimately lead to the person of Jesus.

19. THEY CAME TO BETHLEHEM: A trip from Moab (sixty to seventy-five miles) would have taken about seven to ten days. Having descended about 4,500 feet from Moab into the Jordan Valley, they then ascended 3,750 feet through the hills of Judea.

IS THIS NAOMI: This question most likely reflected the hard life of the last decade and the toll that it had taken on Naomi's appearance.

20. CALL ME MARA: Naomi means "pleasant," while Mara means "bitter." On her return to Judah, Naomi expressed the bitterness in her soul—and

in the process wrongly concluded that God was "testif[ying]" against her (verse 21). But God had not abandoned Naomi, no matter how overwhelming she found her trials to be.

AT THE BEGINNING OF BARLEY HARVEST: Normally the middle to the end of April.

BACK IN JUDAH: *Naomi and Ruth arrive in Judah, and Ruth immediately sets to work gathering food for them both. Then God reveals His loving, sovereign hand.*

2:1. RELATIVE OF NAOMI'S HUSBAND: This man was possibly as close as a brother of Elimelech, but if not, certainly within the tribe or clan.

A MAN OF GREAT WEALTH: Literally "a man of valor" who had unusual capacity to obtain and protect his property.

BOAZ: His name means "in him is strength." He had never married or was a widower.

2. RUTH THE MOABITESS: The author used this phrase repeatedly to show Ruth was actually an outsider—one who had no right to be part of the congregation of Israel *at all*. It is a beautiful picture of God's grace, as He reaches out to those who are outside of salvation—even to those who deserve His grace the least—and brings them into His kingdom.

GLEAN HEADS OF GRAIN: The Mosaic law stipulated that God's people should deliberately leave behind certain portions of any harvest (see Leviticus 19:9–10). This allowed the needy to come through a harvested field and pick up leftover grain or grapes, a process called *gleaning*.

3. SHE HAPPENED TO COME: Here again we see the sovereignty of God at work. From a human perspective, Ruth coincidentally selected the field of Boaz, who coincidentally was Naomi's relative—and coincidentally was rich. But there was no coincidence involved. The Lord was leading Ruth to Boaz, and His plan of blessing extended beyond Ruth's immediate family.

4. BOAZ CAME FROM BETHLEHEM: Here is another detail that appears, from a human perspective, to be mere coincidence. Boaz evidently lived in Bethlehem, and he just happened to choose that particular day to travel to his field to check on the harvest. But once again, it was the Lord's sovereign hand that deliberately orchestrated this historic meeting.

*TWO GODLY CHARACTERS: Boaz and Ruth meet, and each
immediately recognizes godly character in the other person.*

7. SHEAVES: These were bundles of grain stalks tied together for transport
to the threshing floor.

CONTINUED FROM MORNING UNTIL NOW: Ruth was a diligent worker,
laboring tirelessly to provide for her mother-in-law.

THE HOUSE: Likely a temporary shelter built with branches by the side of
the field.

8. MY DAUGHTER: Boaz was approximately the same age as Naomi, about
forty-five to fifty-five years old. He would naturally see Ruth as a daughter,
much like Naomi did.

STAY CLOSE BY MY YOUNG WOMEN: Boaz went above and beyond what
was required of him by the Mosaic law. He was only required to permit Ruth
to glean what was left behind when the harvest was complete, generally after
his workers had left the field. But he urged her to glean while his employees
harvested and pressed her to not move to anyone else's field. Later, he would
instruct his young men to deliberately drop extra grain for her to pick up
(see verses 15–16). Boaz demonstrated the spirit of God's law, being kind to
strangers and caring for widows.

9. YOUNG MEN: The ones who cut the grain with hand sickles.

10. WHY HAVE I FOUND FAVOR IN YOUR EYES: Ruth remained humble,
always remembering she was in Judah only by special accommodation. She
did not have the attitude that the world owed her something, despite the fact
she might have made a legitimate claim on Boaz's generosity because she had
married into his family.

I AM A FOREIGNER: Ruth remained ever mindful that she was an alien
and as such must conduct herself humbly.

11. FULLY REPORTED TO ME: This indicates Naomi's quickness to speak
kindly of Ruth and Boaz's network of influence in Bethlehem.

ALL THAT YOU HAVE DONE FOR YOUR MOTHER-IN-LAW: Ruth's generous character and diligence had earned her a reputation among the Israelites.

12. UNDER WHOSE WINGS YOU HAVE COME FOR REFUGE: Boaz stood
in sharp contrast to Naomi, as he recognized the true nature of God's character. Naomi pictured God as a harsh judge, while Boaz recognized that God

protects and cares for His children just as a mother hen covers her young with her wings—even to the point of sacrificing her own life on their behalf. This picture was perfectly fulfilled when God's Son gave His own life on the cross for our sake.

14. VINEGAR: Sour wine mixed with a little oil was used to quench thirst.

17. EPHAH: This amounts to over one-half bushel, weighing about thirty to forty pounds.

20. HIS KINDNESS: Naomi began to understand God's sovereignty, covenant loyalty, loving-kindness, and mercy toward her, because Ruth—without human direction—had found the near relative Boaz.

ONE OF OUR CLOSE RELATIVES. The great kinsman-redeemer theme of Ruth begins here. A close relative could redeem (1) a family member sold into slavery, (2) land that needed to be sold under economic hardship, and/or (3) the family name by virtue of a levirate marriage. This earthly custom pictures the reality of God the Redeemer doing a greater work by reclaiming those who needed to be spiritually redeemed out of slavery to sin.

22. DO NOT MEET YOU: Ruth the Moabitess would not be treated with such mercy and grace by strangers outside of the family.

23. THE END OF BARLEY HARVEST: Barley harvest usually began about mid-April, and wheat harvest extended to mid-June—a period of intense labor for about two months.

UNLEASHING THE TEXT

1) If you had been in Naomi's position, how would you have responded when your husband and sons died in a foreign land?

_____

_____

_____

_____

2) If you had been in Orpah and Ruth's position, what would you have done when Naomi urged you to return to Moab?

_____

_____

_____

3) What character traits do you see in Ruth? In Boaz? In Naomi?

_____

_____

_____

4) Why did Boaz treat Ruth with so much kindness?

_____

_____

_____

EXPLORING THE MEANING

God works all things together for good in the lives of His children. Naomi endured much grief and suffering, fleeing her native land because of famine, moving to a strange place whose people worshiped false gods, and watching as her husband and two sons died there. From a human perspective, one can easily understand how she would be overcome with sorrow and would feel that the Lord had dealt harshly with her.

Yet the Lord had tremendous blessing in store for her that would outweigh her loss. Her daughter-in-law turned away from the pagan gods of Moab and embraced the true God of Israel. Ruth was providentially brought together with Boaz, a wealthy and influential man in Israel. As we shall see, this would bring blessings that extended far into the future.

God's people are not exempt from sorrow and hardship, and all suffering seems grievous at the time. But we must remember that all things are under the sovereign control of God, and nothing can touch us that God Himself has not approved. He sends discipline and heartache into our lives to purify us and to make us more like Christ, but in the long run the blessings far outweigh the hardships. "And we know that all things work together for good to those who love God, to those who are the called according to His purpose" (Romans 8:28).

The Lord makes His salvation available to all people everywhere. The Moabites were descended from Lot's incestuous relations with his daughters. Balak, a prince of Moab, had even attempted to put a curse on Israel by hiring Balaam (see Numbers 22–25). For these reasons and more, God had forbidden the Moabites from entering the congregation of Israel. In many ways, the people of Moab were outcasts in the eyes of God's people.

But Ruth chose to forsake the gods of Moab and embrace the God of Israel, and in that moment she ceased to be an outcast and became a beloved child of God. She was welcomed into the land of Israel, where she discovered, to her joy, that the Lord had a breathtaking plan for her life and her descendants. He had all the details worked out in advance.

Ruth went from being an outsider with no hope of entering God's presence to being included in the human line of Jesus. In the same way, any sinner who embraces God's salvation through Christ is instantly transformed from despair into joy, from outcast to heir, from death into life. This incomparable grace is available to all, regardless of their background, sins, or past. God welcomes *all* who come to Him in sincere repentance.

God rewards our faithfulness. Orpah and Ruth were faced with a difficult decision: Should they follow Naomi to Judah or return to their families in Moab? Orpah followed what seemed to be the prudent course, returning to Moab in hopes of finding another husband and raising a family. Ruth, however, chose the more difficult path by opting to remain faithful to her mother-in-law. She was not obligated to do so, as her husband had died, yet she took seriously her marital commitment to remain part of her husband's family.

Both Ruth and Boaz demonstrated faithfulness. Ruth was diligent to gather cast-off grain, a task that was lowly in that culture. Boaz fulfilled his duties to the law by permitting Ruth to glean in his field—and then went far beyond what was required in looking after her and Naomi. Both Ruth and Boaz proved faithful in their obedience to God's Word and their loyalty to family.

This is the attitude God desires in all of His children: to serve others out of a heart of humility and sincerity. He calls His people to give with a cheerful heart, to serve one another with a selfless spirit, and to show love without hypocrisy. He Himself set the example by washing His disciples' feet. "'You shall love the Lord your God with all your heart, with all your soul, and with all your mind,'" He taught. "This is the first and great commandment. And the second is like it: 'You shall love your neighbor as yourself.' On these two commandments hang all the Law and the Prophets" (Matthew 22:37–40).

REFLECTING ON THE TEXT

5) Skim through Ruth 1–2 and look for behind-the-scenes evidence of God's sovereign hand. How did He work out all the details for Naomi and Ruth?

_____

_____

_____

6) What losses did Naomi suffer? What blessings did she gain?

_____

_____

_____

7) What sort of treatment should Ruth have expected when she moved to Judah? What did she experience instead? Why?

_____

_____

_____

8) Nothing further is known of Orpah. What does this suggest about her decision to stay in Moab? Why was this a poor decision?

_____

_____

_____

PERSONAL RESPONSE

9) When have you seen God's sovereign hand working to bring blessings out of suffering? What areas of hardship are you experiencing now? What spiritual blessings might God be producing for the future?

_____

_____

_____

10) Is your life characterized by faithfulness to God? In what areas might the Lord want you to be more faithful?

_____

_____

_____

11

THE KINSMAN REDEEMER

Ruth 3:1–4:22

DRAWING NEAR

What does it mean to "redeem" something? What kinds of sacrifices or costs are involved?

_____

_____

_____

THE CONTEXT

Family and heritage were of paramount importance in Old Testament times. A man who had many sons considered himself blessed by God because his family line would increase and prosper through his offspring. Property was an inviolable heritage to a family; a piece of land that one inherited from one's father was to be kept in the family at all costs.

Therefore, it was a terrible tragedy for a man to die without a son, as the inheritance and family name were perpetuated through the male line. It meant the family name would die out, and the ancestral property would go to someone else. In the eyes of the world at large, it was a sign of God's disfavor if a man died without an heir.

For this reason, the law made provision for a "kinsman redeemer," known as the levirate law. This stipulated that a close relative of the dead man could marry the widow on behalf of the deceased. Their firstborn son would take the name of the deceased, and he would inherit all of that man's property. In this way, the family line was continued, and the inheritance remained in the dead man's family.

As we saw in the previous study, all of Naomi's sons had died, and Ruth's late husband had not produced a son. They had already lost the family property through poverty, and the future looked bleak for both women. Unless a close relative was willing to step up and marry Ruth, there was no hope for the family line.

Yet the Lord had it all under control. He was already working to bring together Ruth and Boaz through His divine sovereignty. In this study, we will consider the person of Boaz himself and look at what he undertook when he became Ruth's kinsman redeemer. In doing so, we will gain some better insight into the person and work of Jesus Christ.

KEYS TO THE TEXT

Read Ruth 3:1–4:22, noting the key words and phrases indicated below.

A BRIGHTER FUTURE: Encouraged by Ruth's day in Boaz's field, Naomi instructs Ruth in the way she should go about ensuring a brighter future for both of them.

3:1. SECURITY FOR YOU: Naomi felt responsible for Ruth's future husband and home.

2. WINNOWING BARLEY TONIGHT: Winnowing (tossing grain into the air to separate the grain from the chaff) normally occurred in late afternoon when the Mediterranean winds prevailed. Sifting and bagging the grain would have carried over past dark, and Boaz might have remained all night to guard the grain from theft.

THRESHING FLOOR: Usually a large, hard area of earth or stone on the downwind (east) side of the village where threshing took place.

3. WASH YOURSELF AND ANOINT YOURSELF: Naomi instructed Ruth to look her best and propose marriage to Boaz by utilizing an ancient Near

Eastern custom. The older, gracious Boaz would not have initiated such a marriage proposal with a younger woman.

7. HIS HEART WAS CHEERFUL: Boaz had a sense of well-being, which was most readily explained by the full harvest in contrast to previous years of famine.

9. TAKE YOUR MAIDSERVANT: Ruth righteously appealed to Boaz, using the language of Boaz's earlier prayer, to marry her according to the levirate custom.

10. YOU HAVE SHOWN MORE KINDNESS: Boaz commended Ruth's loyalty to Naomi, to the Lord, and even to himself.

GO AFTER YOUNG MEN: Ruth demonstrated moral excellence in that she did not engage in immorality, did not remarry outside the family, and had appealed for levirate redemption to an older, godly man.

KNOW THAT YOU ARE A VIRTUOUS WOMAN: In all respects, Ruth personified excellence. This same language was used of Boaz (see Ruth 2:1), making them the perfectly matched couple for an exemplary marriage.

A SLIGHT GLITCH: Boaz agrees to marry Ruth according to the levirate custom, but there is a problem. A closer family member than himself exists to fulfill this role.

12. A RELATIVE CLOSER THAN I: Boaz righteously deferred to someone else who was nearer in relationship to Elimelech. The nearer relative may have been Boaz's older brother, or Boaz may have been his cousin. The fact that the neighbor women said "there is a son born to Naomi" (Ruth 4:17) at Obed's birth suggests the brother or cousin relationship to Elimelech.

13. I WILL PERFORM THE DUTY: Boaz willingly accepted Ruth's proposal if the nearer relative was unable or unwilling to exercise his levirate duty.

AS THE LORD LIVES: This was the most solemn and binding oath an Israelite could vow.

14. LAY AT HIS FEET UNTIL MORNING: According to the text, no immorality occurred. Boaz even insisted on no appearance of evil.

15. SIX EPHAHS: The Hebrew text gives no standard of measurement—the translators inserted *ephah* only as a possibility. However, six ephahs would weigh about two hundred pounds, which would have been far too much for Ruth to carry home in her shawl. Therefore, it is more reasonable that six *seahs*

is intended here (sixty to eighty pounds), which would have been twice the amount Ruth had previously gleaned.

18. THIS DAY: Naomi knew that Boaz was a man of integrity and would fulfill his promise with a sense of urgency. She and Ruth needed to wait on the Lord to work through Boaz.

SEEKING A REDEEMER: Boaz now travels to the city to determine whether the closer relative is willing to exercise his levirate duty on behalf of Naomi's family.

4:1. BOAZ WENT UP TO THE GATE: These events took place after the harvest was completed.

THE CLOSE RELATIVE OF WHOM BOAZ HAD SPOKEN: The Hebrew word translated "close relative" refers to a person who acted as protector of the family rights. He could be called on by family members to perform a number of duties: (1) buy back property the family had sold, (2) provide an heir for a deceased brother by marrying his widow (these two situations were facing Boaz), (3) buy back a family member who had been sold into slavery due to poverty, or (4) avenge a relative's murder by killing the murderer. This same Hebrew word is used of God in the book of Isaiah: "You shall know that I, the LORD, am your Savior and your Redeemer, the Mighty One of Jacob" (60:16). God is our "Close Relative," our "Kinsman Redeemer."

4. BUY IT BACK: Naomi's poverty had forced her to sell a piece of land that was part of her family inheritance. The people of Israel were not permitted to permanently sell family land, for the land itself ultimately belongs to the Lord. "The land shall not be sold permanently, for the land is Mine; for you are strangers and sojourners with Me" (Leviticus 25:23).

5. TO PERPETUATE THE NAME OF THE DEAD: In this somewhat complicated transaction, Boaz told his relative he was obligated to do more than just purchase the land if he took on the role of kinsman redeemer—he also would be obligated to marry Ruth. The principle was that a family line would die out if a man died without a son, so the kinsman redeemer was required to marry the widow and raise up a son who would carry on that family name. The firstborn son would receive the deceased man's inheritance, thus keeping property in the same family.

NOT WILLING TO PAY THE PRICE: The closer relative is willing to buy back the property but not to marry Ruth, which allows Boaz to become the family's kinsman redeemer.

6. LEST I RUIN MY OWN INHERITANCE: This unnamed relative evidently was willing to purchase the family field but not to marry Ruth. His reasons are not entirely clear, but it is possible he was unwilling to buy the field only to have it pass on to a different family line. (The first son born to him and Ruth would bear the name of Ruth's first husband, rather than his own.)

10. THAT THE NAME OF THE DEAD MAY NOT BE CUT OFF: The concept of being "cut off" was of profound importance to Israel. It meant to be cast out of the camp, to be deprived of access to God's presence. (Remember the Lord's presence was visibly with the camp of Israel during their wilderness wanderings, prior to arriving in Canaan.) In a metaphorical sense, the name of Ruth's deceased husband would be similarly cut off, lost to all memory among God's people. This would be prevented, however, if Boaz married Ruth and raised a son in the dead man's name.

12. LIKE THE HOUSE OF PEREZ: The people at the gate blessed Boaz and Ruth and asked the Lord to make them fruitful with offspring. They mentioned Rachel and Leah as significant examples in Israel's history, as they were the wives of Jacob who bore most of his sons (the fathers of the twelve tribes of Israel). It is interesting that Perez was also singled out in this list, as he was technically an illegitimate son born of an incestuous union (see Genesis 38).

14. WHO HAS NOT LEFT YOU THIS DAY WITHOUT A CLOSE RELATIVE: The Lord Himself had blessed Ruth by providing a "close relative" or redeemer in the person of Boaz. The Lord blesses all mankind in a far greater way by providing us with the true Redeemer, our greatest Close Relative, Jesus Christ.

15. WHO IS BETTER TO YOU THAN SEVEN SONS: Naomi had misunderstood the character of God previously when she publicly proclaimed, "The hand of the LORD has gone out against me!" (Ruth 1:13). Now she saw that God had never abandoned her or turned His back on her—quite the opposite, in fact. In the end, she was blessed far beyond the losses she had suffered, as made more poignant by the fact that she nursed the grandfather of David.

17. OBED: Obed's son Jesse was the father of David.

GOING DEEPER

Read Galatians 4:3–7, noting the key words and phrases indicated below.

JESUS IS OUR KINSMAN REDEEMER: God used the experiences of Ruth and Boaz to paint a picture of His ultimate plan: to redeem mankind as His own inheritance.

4:3. IN BONDAGE: The human race was in bondage to sin and death, "the elements of the world," and there was no hope of redemption prior to Christ. We had been "cut off" from God, and there was no possibility of being reinstated into God's grace.

4. BORN UNDER THE LAW: Boaz and the unnamed "close relative" present an important contrast. The unnamed man was unwilling to submit himself to the levirate law and unwilling to become Ruth's kinsman redeemer, because it would have cost him something. Boaz, on the other hand, willingly submitted to his responsibilities and became Ruth's kinsman redeemer. Jesus is the Creator of the universe, God the Son, the Word made flesh, the only human ever to live a sinless life—yet He willingly submitted Himself to becoming a man, born under the law, in order to redeem us. Being "under the law" includes the fact that Christ willingly allowed Himself to face temptation on our behalf—yet without sin—and He submitted to the ultimate curse of mankind by voluntarily dying on the cross.

5. TO REDEEM THOSE WHO WERE UNDER THE LAW: As those who had violated God's law, we had no hope of eternal life and no prospect of being reconciled to God. We were dead in our sins and doomed to be eternally cut off from the Father. Yet God Himself provided the way: He became our Kinsman Redeemer, and through Christ we are no longer cut off but are redeemed into eternal life and fellowship with God.

ADOPTION AS SONS: When we receive Christ as our Redeemer, we are "born again" into the family of Jesus and inherit all that He owns—which is to say, all that there is in eternity. We receive the name of Christ and even develop His character. We come to look and act just like our Redeemer through the Holy Spirit's refining work.

6. ABBA, FATHER: *Abba* is a term of affection similar to our word *Daddy*. Through the Holy Spirit, we are able to communicate with God in a

new way, crying out to Him, "Daddy!" Christ's work of redemption takes us from being cut off and fatherless into a deep relationship of intimacy with our eternal Father.

7. YOU ARE NO LONGER A SLAVE BUT A SON: We are given, free of charge, an eternal inheritance and an everlasting family. Boaz redeemed Ruth's inheritance with gold, but Christ redeemed us with something infinitely more valuable: His own precious blood. "You were not redeemed with corruptible things, like silver or gold, from your aimless conduct received by tradition from your fathers, but with the precious blood of Christ, as of a lamb without blemish and without spot" (1 Peter 1:18–19).

UNLEASHING THE TEXT

1) If you had been in Boaz's place, how would you have responded when Ruth told you that you were her close relative?

_____

_____

_____

2) If you had been in Ruth's place, how would you have responded to Boaz's actions? How would you have felt when the other man refused to become your redeemer?

_____

_____

_____

3) Why did the other relative refuse to become Ruth's kinsman redeemer? Why did Boaz accept the responsibility? What do these responses reveal about the character of God?

_____

_____

_____

4) What did it cost Boaz to become the kinsman redeemer? What did Ruth gain? What did Naomi gain?

_____

_____

_____

EXPLORING THE MEANING

Mankind has no hope apart from Christ. Ruth's first husband had died without producing a son and heir, which meant his family line would cease to exist. This was a terrible fate in Old Testament times and suggested that God Himself had cut off that man's family. There was no hope of changing that situation, as Ruth by herself could hardly produce a son in her husband's family line. The only solution was to have a relative of her dead husband marry her and produce a son in the late man's name—a situation that was completely out of Ruth's control.

The Bible makes it abundantly clear that the human race is cut off from God in its sinful, unredeemed condition. God detests sin and cannot permit it in His presence. Yet every descendant of Adam has sinned. We are born with a sinful nature, and nothing can ever remove it, "for all have sinned and fall short of the glory of God" (Romans 3:23). "All we like sheep have gone astray; we have turned, every one, to his own way; and the LORD has laid on Him the iniquity of us all" (Isaiah 53:6).

But God had planned from before the foundation of the world to redeem mankind to Himself. He knew that no descendant of Adam could redeem the fallen race, because every person born from Adam's line would inherit his nature—the *sin* nature. The only way mankind could be redeemed was through the Son of God, Jesus Christ, who was born of a virgin. Jesus committed no sin, yet He died voluntarily on the cross, taking on Himself the punishment due to Adam's sinful race.

Jesus is our Kinsman Redeemer. Ruth was bereft of property and kin and doomed to a life of poverty. Her only hope lay in the hands of a stranger who had little to gain from a marriage to her. Yet Boaz rose voluntarily to the call of duty and took upon himself the full responsibility of caring for his relatives. What's more, he was in love with Ruth! He did not marry her in a grumbling spirit of obligation but with a joyful, enthusiastic attitude.

Boaz provides us with a small picture of Christ in His role as our Redeemer. We were without hope, without inheritance, without a future, and there was nothing we could do to change that grim picture. Yet Jesus took upon Himself the full responsibility of caring for us, and He is preparing a place for us as His bride for all eternity. He did this voluntarily, not out of any compulsion—even to the point of willingly dying on the cross.

And best of all, He loves us! Jesus was willing to die on the cross because He yearned for our fellowship and longed to be reunited with His fallen creatures. He knows us intimately, even to numbering the very hairs of our heads, and He delights in our company. He is our joyful Redeemer, the One who bought us back with His own blood—and did so willingly.

Christ's redemption is free to us but costly to God. The role of kinsman redeemer involved a heavy responsibility. It almost certainly included some financial burden and could even put a man at risk of his own life. One of his responsibilities might be to see justice done for a murder, and might have called him to take the life of the murderer with his own hands. Boaz's relative was unwilling to pay the cost of redeeming Ruth because it would have had a negative impact on his own inheritance. But Boaz did not hesitate to pay whatever cost was required because of his great love for Ruth.

Jesus knew even before He went to the cross that He would be called on to pay the ultimate cost to become our Redeemer. Like Boaz, He was under no obligation to pay that cost, for He had never sinned. Nevertheless, He chose voluntarily to pay it with His own sinless life, fulfilling the Redeemer's role of putting to death the enemy of mankind: death itself.

Ruth did nothing to attain the love and redemption of Boaz. He paid the full price, and she received it simply by saying, "I do." We too receive God's redemption freely, at no cost to ourselves, for the price has been paid in full at the cross by Jesus Christ. By embracing Him in faith, we receive the priceless redemption of eternal life—a redemption that cost God the life of His only Son.

REFLECTING ON THE TEXT

5) In what ways has Boaz's faithfulness influenced the world?

_____

_____

_____

6) How do Boaz's actions as a kinsman redeemer point to the redemption of Christ?

_____

_____

_____

7) What does it mean that Jesus is our Kinsman Redeemer? What does that role involve?

_____

_____

_____

8) Why did Jesus voluntarily become our Kinsman Redeemer? What did it cost Him? What did we gain?

_____

_____

_____

Personal Response

9) Have you embraced Jesus Christ as your Redeemer and Lord? If not, what is preventing you?

_____

_____

_____

10) If you have accepted Christ as your Savior, what does that mean long-term? What inheritance do you have? What guarantees do you have?

_____

_____

_____

12

Reviewing Key Principles

Drawing Near

As you look back at each of the studies from Joshua, Judges, and Ruth, what is the one thing that stood out to you the most? What is one new perspective you have learned?

_____

_____

_____

The Context

We have covered a large span of time in Israel's history in the previous eleven studies, and we have met many memorable people along the way. The encouraging thing to recognize is that these were real people, and we have seen them just as they were—blemishes and all. What's more, they were confronted by real life. Sometimes they faced life's more dramatic events, and sometimes they faced everyday routine.

Many of these individuals proved faithful to God, but some did not. Yet one theme that has remained constant throughout is that God is *always* faithful. Some of the characters we've met (such as Ruth) trusted Him implicitly, while some (such as Samson) were prone to trust only themselves, but God remained faithful to His word and His people from beginning to end. If you come away with only one thought from these studies, let it be this: God is *always* faithful.

Here are a few of the major themes we have found. There are many more that we don't have room to reiterate, so take some time to review the earlier studies—or, better still, to meditate on the passages of Scripture we have covered. Ask the Holy Spirit to give you wisdom and insight into His Word. He will not refuse.

EXPLORING THE MEANING

God cannot be deceived. Prior to the Israelites taking Jericho, the Lord had told Joshua to not touch any of the possessions in the city (see Joshua 6:18–19). Achan understood this command, but he believed he could take just a few small items without any consequences. He then buried those stolen items in the ground beneath his tent—an excellent hiding place if ever there was one. Achan and his family actually believed they could hide their sin from God.

The fact is, they did succeed in hiding their sin from other people. It would appear that nobody outside of Achan's family was aware of the stolen property, and Joshua confidently led the army into battle in the belief that all was well. But the Lord knew what Achan had done, and He was not willing to overlook the transgression. *All* sin, no matter how small in the world's eyes, is an abhorrent offense in the eyes of God.

It may be easy to hide our sins from the people around us, but we can never hide them from God. He calls us to purify our lives from every sin and confess them openly before Him. "Do not be deceived, God is not mocked; for whatever a man sows, that he will also reap. For he who sows to his flesh will of the flesh reap corruption, but he who sows to the Spirit will of the Spirit reap everlasting life" (Galatians 6:7–8).

Covetousness is the same as idolatry. Achan was motivated by covetousness. He confessed it was his own eyes that led him into sin: he *saw* beautiful things in Jericho, and he coveted them in his heart. What he coveted, he also took; and what he took, he ultimately hid.

It is not a sin to admire beautiful things, but it is a sin to *covet* them. To covet is to lust for something—to fix one's mind on material possessions or financial gain. We begin to covet when we long to possess something that does not belong to us, or we become absorbed with getting what we don't have. Achan did not sin when he noticed that the garment in Jericho was lovely; he sinned when he determined that he had to own it, in spite of God's prohibitions.

When we covet, we fix our hearts on material goods, and those desires begin to drive our thoughts, actions, and attitudes. In this way, the thing we covet becomes like a god to us—an "idol" in our lives. The Lord wants us to fix our eyes on Him alone and turn them away from the things of this world. "Put to death . . . covetousness, which is idolatry" (Colossians 3:5).

God can literally move heaven and earth to accomplish His purposes. Or, to speak more accurately, the Lord will cause the earth and heavens (the atmosphere) to *not* move. In order for the sun to "stand still," as we read in Joshua 10, the earth itself would have had to stop revolving on its axis—and this is evidently what the Lord did for the Israelites that momentous day. He literally caused the earth to stop for a period of hours simply so that His people might have victory in battle.

The Lord went beyond even this "earthshaking" miracle when He moved heaven itself—the abode of God—to send His Son to earth as a man. He temporarily set aside the laws of biology and caused a virgin to become pregnant with the Son of God. More than this, He permitted His Holy One to take on the sin of mankind; He caused the One who is Life to taste death; He subjected the Creator to the whims of those He had created. He did all this so we might be reconciled with Himself.

If God was willing to do all of this for the sake of sinful people in the past, He will certainly prove faithful in meeting our present needs. Some problems may be too great to resolve in our power, but there is no problem too great for God. He will move heaven and earth to show Himself faithful to His people.

Do not be afraid, but be strong and of good courage. This commandment appears frequently in the book of Joshua—usually at times when there seemed to be genuine cause for fear. Prior to one battle, the army of Israel had marched all night long, uphill, carrying all their gear for battle (see Joshua 10). They arrived to face not one but five enemy armies, and they were tired before the battle even began. Yet the Lord commanded His people to not give in to fear.

Fear is the enemy of God's people. It moves us away from faith and toward disobedience. In a previous encounter, the people of Israel had arrived at the

Jordan River, ready to take possession of the Promised Land. But their spies had brought back a discouraging report: there were giants in the land—and fortified cities! The people yielded to fear and disobeyed the Lord. As a result, that entire generation was doomed to die in the wilderness without entering the land of Canaan (see Numbers 13–14).

We are commanded to resist fear, which demonstrates fear is something we can master. This is done by shifting our focus away from the situation that threatens us and focusing on the Lord who redeems us. He is absolutely sovereign over all our affairs, and He is completely faithful to save His people. If He was willing to make the sun stand still for Israel's army, He will be willing to intervene in our lives as well.

Do not fall into a cycle of sin and repentance. The people of Israel disobeyed the Lord's command to drive out the Canaanites, which led them into idolatry and immorality. The Lord responded by sending hardship on them as a form of discipline and to urge them to return to obedience and purity. The oppression of enemies and other calamities forced Israel to repent and return to the Lord, and He graciously sent judges to lead them back to obedience. But after a time, the people lost interest in the things of God and soon fell into sin again.

This cycle was not pleasing to God. He wants His people to obey Him willingly and worship Him voluntarily, with whole hearts. God will send discipline into our lives to make us purer and more like Christ, but His desire is for us to obey Him out of love and gratitude rather than by the compulsion of hardship. It is a mark of spiritual maturity to obey God's Word simply because we know it pleases and glorifies the Father.

Christians are to obey God's commands, not to negotiate for a "better deal." Barak was the leader of Israel's military, and as such he was likely accustomed to having his commands obeyed without argument. After all, a good soldier never talks back to a commanding officer—he carries out the commands without comment. It was all the more startling, therefore, when Barak countermanded the direct orders of his Commanding Officer—God Himself.

Picture a general commanding a soldier to move into battle and the soldier responding, "I will go into battle only if you come with me; if you will not come with me, I won't go." That soldier's career would be short. Yet how much more audacious it is when we try to find ways around simple obedience to God's

Word! We do this when we obey only partway, or tell ourselves we will begin to obey tomorrow, or ignore the promptings of the Holy Spirit.

The Lord wants His people to obey His Word with willing hearts—not by compulsion. We cannot experience the Lord's full blessing in our lives unless we willingly obey His commands. As Deborah sang, "When the people willingly offer themselves, bless the LORD!" (Judges 5:2).

Ask God for guidance, but don't put Him to the test. The Scriptures abound with men and women who were faced with difficult circumstances or decisions and turned to the Lord for guidance. Jesus urged His disciples to seek the Father's will in all things, teaching them to pray, "Your will be done on earth as it is in heaven" (Matthew 6:10). Today, Christians receive the indwelling of the Holy Spirit, whose role in part is to guide us into all truth (see John 16:13). There is no excuse for putting God to the test in order to receive direction.

Of course, this was not what Gideon was really doing when he put out his fleeces in Judges 6. The Lord had *already* given him guidance and told him exactly what to do—but Gideon was afraid. He feared the Lord would not keep His promises, so he sought miraculous verification of God's faithfulness. The Lord had repeatedly proven Himself faithful throughout Israel's history—parting the Jordan River for them to cross, bringing down the walls of Jericho, giving His people one victory after another against powerful enemies—and Gideon should have rested in faith that He would keep His word once again.

Modern Christians also have a record of God's faithfulness through the ages. We learn of it throughout the Bible as we read the testimonies of those who walked with God in the past. If we live in light of God's Word and obey the truth He has revealed to us in Scripture, we can do so with confidence, knowing God will be faithful in the present just as He has been in the past.

Jesus is our Kinsman Redeemer. Ruth was doomed to a life of poverty, bereft of property and kin. There was nothing she could do to change her circumstances, and her only hope lay in the hands of a stranger who had little to gain from a marriage to her. Yet Boaz voluntarily rose to the call of duty and took on himself the full responsibility of caring for his relatives. What's more, he was in love with Ruth! He did not marry her in a grumbling spirit of obligation but with a joyful, enthusiastic attitude.

Boaz provides us with a small picture of Christ in His role as our Redeemer. We were without hope, without inheritance, without a future, and there was nothing we could do to change that grim picture. Yet Jesus took on Himself the full responsibility of caring for us, and He is preparing a place for us as His bride for all eternity. He did this voluntarily, not out of any compulsion—even to the point of willingly dying on the cross.

Best of all, Jesus loves us! He was willing to die on the cross because He yearned for our fellowship and longed to be reunited with His fallen creatures. He knows us intimately, even to numbering the very hairs of our heads, and He delights in our company. He is our joyful Redeemer, the One who bought us back with His own blood—and freely chose to do so.

UNLEASHING THE TEXT

1) Which of the concepts or principles in this study have you found to be the most encouraging? Why?

_____

_____

_____

2) Which of the concepts or principles have you found most challenging? Why?

_____

_____

_____

_____

3) What aspects of "walking with God" are you already doing in your life? Which areas need strengthening?

_____

_____

_____

4) To which of the characters that we've studied have you most been able to relate? How might you emulate that person in your own life?

_____

_____

_____

PERSONAL RESPONSE

5) Have you taken a definite stand for Jesus Christ? Have you accepted His free gift of salvation? If not, what is preventing you from doing so?

_____

_____

_____

6) In what areas of your life have you been most convicted during this study? What exact things will you do to address these convictions? Be specific.

_____

_____

_____

7) What have you learned about the character of God during this study? How has this insight affected your worship or prayer life?

_____

_____

_____

8) What are some specific things you want to see God do in your life in the coming month? What are some things you intend to change in your own life during that time? (Return to this list in one month and hold yourself accountable to fulfill these things.)

_____

_____

_____

If you would like to continue in your study of the Old Testament, read the next title in this series: *1 Samuel: The Lives of Samuel and Saul.*

ALSO AVAILABLE

In this study, John MacArthur guides readers through an in-depth look at the historical period beginning with God's calling of Moses, continuing through the giving of the Ten Commandments, and concluding with the Israelites' preparations to enter the Promised Land. This study includes close-up examinations of Aaron, Caleb, Joshua, Balaam and Balak, as well as careful considerations of doctrinal themes such as "Complaints and Rebellion" and "Following God's Law."

The MacArthur Bible Studies provide intriguing examinations of the whole of Scripture. Each guide incorporates extensive commentary, detailed observations on overriding themes, and probing questions to help you study the Word of God with guidance from John MacArthur.

ALSO AVAILABLE

In this study, John MacArthur guides readers through an in-depth look at this historical period beginning with the miraculous birth of Samuel, continuing through Saul's crowning as Israel's first king, and concluding with his tragic death. Studies include close-up examinations of Hannah, Eli, Saul, David, and Jonathan, as well as careful considerations of doctrinal themes such as "Slaying a Giant" and "Respecting God's Anointed."

The MacArthur Bible Studies provide intriguing examinations of the whole of Scripture. Each guide incorporates extensive commentary, detailed observations on overriding themes, and probing questions to help you study the Word of God with guidance from John MacArthur.

ALSO AVAILABLE

In this study, John MacArthur guides readers through an in-depth look at the historical period beginning with David's struggle to establish his throne, continuing through his sin and repentance, and concluding with the tragic rebellion of his son Absalom. Studies include close-up examinations of Joab, Amnon, Tamar, Absalom, and others, as well as careful considerations of doctrinal themes such as "Obedience and Blessing" and being a "Man After God's Own Heart."

The MacArthur Bible Studies provide intriguing examinations of the whole of Scripture. Each guide incorporates extensive commentary, detailed observations on overriding themes, and probing questions to help you study the Word of God with guidance from John MacArthur.

ALSO AVAILABLE

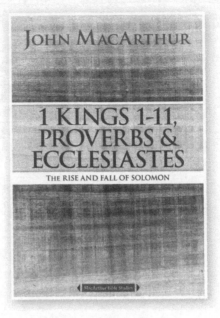

In this study, John MacArthur guides readers through an in-depth look at the historical period beginning with Solomon's ascent to the throne and continuing through his tragic end. Studies include close-up examinations of the vital importance of wisdom—with portraits of the wise woman, the foolish sluggard, and others in the book of Proverbs—and careful considerations of doctrinal themes such as "True Wisdom from God" and "A Time for Everything."

The MacArthur Bible Studies provide intriguing examinations of the whole of Scripture. Each guide incorporates extensive commentary, detailed observations on overriding themes, and probing questions to help you study the Word of God with guidance from John MacArthur.